Real Estate

(2 Books in 1)

John James

Published By: John James

Copyright © All rights reserved

No part of this publication may be copied, reproduced in any format, by any means electronic or otherwise, without prior consent from the copyright owner and publisher of this book.

Real Estate Investing:
The Ultimate Beginners' Guide to Real Estate Investing

Introduction 8

Chapter 1: Getting into Real Estate Investing ... 10

Chapter 2: How Market Conditions Can Determine Your Investment 15

Chapter 3: How to Find Properties to Make You Money in Real Estate 20

Chapter 4: How to Finance Your Investment ... 29

Chapter 5: How to Purchase Your First Property in Real Estate 36

Chapter 6: How Brokers and Property Managers Can Make Your Job Easier 41

Chapter 7: Protecting Your Assets 46

Chapter 8: How to Handle Your Lease When Renting out Properties 50

Chapter 9: How to Avoid Common Mistakes ... 56

Conclusion 62

Real Estate Investing:
The AdvancedGuide to Real Estate Investing

Introduction 66

Chapter 1: Real Estate vs. the Stock Market 68

Chapter 2: Attracting Lenders 81

Chapter 3: Protecting Your Assets 91

Chapter 4: Direct Ownership Real Estate Investment 99

Chapter 5: Real Estate Investment Groups and Limited Partnerships 117

Chapter 6: Real Estate Investment Trusts 120

Conclusion 124

Real Estate Investing

The Ultimate Beginners' Guide to Real Estate Investing

© Copyright 2018 by John James

All rights reserved.

The following eBook is reproduced below with the goal of providing information that is as accurate and reliable as possible. Regardless, purchasing this eBook can be seen as consent to the fact that both the publisher and the author of this book are in no way experts on the topics discussed within and that any recommendations or suggestions that are made herein are for entertainment purposes only. Professionals should be consulted as needed prior to undertaking any of the action endorsed herein.

This declaration is deemed fair and valid by both the American Bar Association and the Committee of Publishers Association and is legally binding throughout the United States.

Furthermore, the transmission, duplication or reproduction of any of the following work including specific information will be considered an illegal act irrespective of whether it is done electronically or in print. This extends to creating a secondary or tertiary copy of the work or a recorded copy and is only allowed with express written consent from the Publisher. All additional rights reserved.

The information in the following pages is broadly considered to be a truthful and accurate account of facts and, as such, any inattention, use or misuse of the information in question by the reader will render any resulting actions solely under their purview. There are no scenarios in which the publisher or the original author of this work can be in any fashion deemed liable for any hardship or damages that may befall them after undertaking information described herein.

Additionally, the information in the following pages is intended only for informational purposes and should thus be thought of as universal. As befitting its nature, it is presented without assurance regarding its prolonged validity or interim quality. Trademarks that are mentioned are done without written consent and can in no way be considered an endorsement from the trademark holder.

Introduction

Congratulations on downloading this book and thank you for doing so.

The following chapters will discuss everything that you need to know in order to get started with investing in real estate. This is a great way to make some money and have a lot of fun at the same time. And there are so many options that you can make in this investment that you could easily diversify your whole portfolio and still keep it inside of this market.

This guidebook is going to take some time to look at how to work in real estate. We will talk about how to get started in this industry, how to find the funding that your investment needs, how to work with a property manager and a real estate broker, how to pick out the lease for your investment, and so much more. There are many aspects that come with working in real estate and it often depends on what kind of property you are planning on using and whether you would like to flip that property or rent it out to others. This guidebook will help you out no matter what you plan to do with this investment.

When you are ready to start putting your money to work for you and making a profit in the real estate market, make sure to check out this guidebook and learn everything that you need in order to get started today.

There are plenty of books on this subject on the market, thanks again for choosing this one! Every effort was made to ensure it is full of as much useful information as possible, please enjoy!

Chapter 1

Getting into Real Estate Investing

While you have a lot of choices to go with when you are ready to start investing your money, real estate can be one of the best options. There are many choices that you can make when you are getting into real estate and there are ways to make money whether the market is doing well or hitting a slump. Each choice is going to provide you with some unique challenges and varying amounts of profit. There is some risk that comes with going into real estate investing and it is going to take some hard work to see results, but there is nothing like working in real estate. Let's take a look at some of the different investment options that you can go with when you are ready to go into real estate.

Residential real estate

The first investment that you can choose is to work with families and individuals who are looking for a place to live. You will offer your property as a rental to them and earn an income from what these families and individuals pay. There are many different types of residential real estate and each one will have a different amount of work and a different amount of profit along the way. Some of the residential properties that you can consider include houses, vacation homes, apartments, and townhomes.

You will find that each one has some benefits. Homes can be popular because there are usually families who will rent them out and most families will stay around for at least a few years, helping you to get a steady stream of income. But some investors like to go with apartments because these can generate more income since they hold more people at once.

Commercial real estate

This is going to include options like office buildings and other similar spaces. When you go into commercial real estate, you will need to find funding to help you construct buildings that will have individual offices for companies and businesses to purchase. While a company is using the building, they will pay you rent. Often these buildings are going to come with leases that are meant to last a few years because most businesses want to get a good deal and do not want to move frequently. This may cost a little more to get started, but it can provide you with a steady stream of income.

Industrial real estate

The next option that you can go with is known as industrial real estate. This one is going to include investments like distribution centers, storage units, and car washes. It can include any kind of real estate that is going to be built for a special purpose and will generate income for the customers who are using the facility. You must remember that these have bigger upfront costs, but the revenue stream is going to be really steady and you will not have to add in a lot of work along the way to keep them going.

Retail real estate

With these investments, you are going to work with options like strip malls, shopping malls, and retail storefronts. There are a lot of businesses willing to pay rent for these spaces, especially if you can place that retail space in an area that has a lot of high traffic. Sometimes the lease is going to include a monthly payment from the tenants, although you can create a lease that will give you a percentage of the sales that your tenants earn while they are in your building. The second option can be nice if you place the building in a good area and your tenants make a lot of money.

These retail spaces are expensive to get started because you need to purchase a lot of land in a busy area and the building is usually pretty big as well. But if you get the right kind of space, you will be able to add in several tenants to that building and earn a bigger income. You can also have some choice in the size of the retail space that you want to go with in order to help determine how much you want to spend and how many tenants you will be able to get into the building.

Mixed use real estate

A good option to go with when you want to make money in real estate is to work with mixed use real estate. This is when you combine a few of the categories above into one project. You must have some good assets to make this work, but they bring out an amazing return on investment if you are able to get people to rent out the building.

An example of doing this is when you invest in building a mixed office building that will hold your main tenants and then you have it surrounded by some retail shops. You would be able to rent it all out. You can even make office buildings with a few stories to rent out more offices or to rent out as apartments. Turn the retail spaces into restaurants, gyms, grocery stores, and so on, and you can really fill up the spaces in no time.

Flipping homes

If you do not feel that holding on to a property and renting it out to other companies or individuals is the right option for your investment needs, it may be a good idea to consider flipping homes. When flipping homes, you do not have to hold on to a building or be a landlord. To make it work, you will need to find a property that is in a good area and for a good price. Usually there is some reason why the property is being offered way under value. Sometimes it is that way because it needs a ton of work, but sometimes you can find one that will only need a bit of work and will be easy to flip.

Flipping a home can turn out to be a tricky investment. While you own that property, you are going to be responsible for making the monthly payments, taking care of insurance, fixing up the home, and any other payments that will come with maintaining the home. This is why it's important to get a good deal on the home and pick out a decent home that you will actually be able to sell later on. Once you purchase the home, you need to make sure that you are able to keep your costs as low as possible and that you can fix it up quickly, so it can get back on the market in no time. The better you are able to stick with these goals the more money you will be able to make. Those who are good at flipping homes will be able to make a lot of money with this investment.

Real estate investing is a great opportunity because it offers so many options for you to choose from. Based on your personal preferences when it comes to investing and how much risk you would like to take, there are different options that can help you get the return on investment you want. Before getting into the market, consider some of these real estate investment types so that you can come up with the winning strategy.

Chapter 2

How Market Conditions Can Determine Your Investment

Many new investors are excited to get started in real estate. They may hear about others who have gotten into this investment and made a lot of money in the process. But before you decide to jump into this investment, it is important that you understand how it works. And the first step is to learn how the market in your area is, so you can make smart decisions.

There are various different markets when it comes to the real estate market. There will be certain times when people are actively searching for homes and you will find that house prices are really high. This is when you will want to consider selling a property or adjusting your rental prices to get the most money possible. Then there are times when the demand for homes is low. This can be a good time to purchase a home because you are more likely to get a good discount on the price. These different phases can happen throughout the year, but often you will want to watch out for the overall trends from one year to another.

There are many times when the market conditions around the real estate industry are going to really influence when you should make purchases, when you are able to sell, and so much more. Each market is going to go through these cycles, no matter how great the area is. There is not always going to be a high demand for homes and you may enter into a cycle where selling homes can be hard. If you happen to purchase a home during these downtimes and they don't reverse quickly, you at least have the option of using your property for rent money to offset some of the costs until the market turns around.

Now, it can be confusing as a beginner to determine when you should get into the market to help you to make the most money and to make sure of the market cycle. Remember that you are able to consider this type of investment no matter what type of market cycle you are in because it is always going to go in a cycle that you can use to your advantage. Some of the different parts of the market cycle that you should learn to recognize to help you make the right decisions on this investment include:

- The peak: The peak is going to be when prices are at an all-time high. At this time, the inventory of available properties is going to be low, which is why the high demand raises the prices so much. In fact, there are often so many interested buyers that a single home, even if it is not in the best shape, will have more than one offer on it. As an investor, this is not the time for you to enter the market because you will pay way more for the home than you will be able to make off it later on.

However, if you already own a home and have finished fixing it up, this is an amazing time to sell it.

- The tipping point: This is the point where home prices are too high and the demand for homes is starting to go down. The prices are going to start falling, which will allow the prices to compensate for the high prices and the overbuilding that occurred in the other part of the cycle. There are times when foreclosure rates are going to go up and some homeowners will have some issues with paying their mortgage because the payments are too high. And then these homeowners will have some issues with selling their home because the value of the home is less than they owe and there are not many interested buyers.
- The decline: This part of the cycle is where the prices of the homes in your area are going to continue to fall. You may notice that you are in this phase when you see many foreclosures going on in the market. People are scared about purchasing homes right now because they do not want to make a purchase that they are not able to afford. With all the foreclosures, there is going to be a lot of inventory on the market that will drive the prices down even further.
- The bottom: This is where the home prices are going to start to even out quite a bit. This part of the cycle will show the lowest prices of the entire thing. If you are looking to get into the

market, this is the point where you would want to purchase a property or two because you will get a huge discount. There are many homeowners who are desperate to sell their homes and get at least something out of the deal. You will have a lot of inventory to look through and you will be able to get a good price, which will save you money and help increase your profits later on.

- The climb: The bottom is not going to last forever. There will be a time when buyers will start to gain more confidence in the market and they will start looking for homes to purchase again. This will help add more sales in real estate in the area and can result in less inventory. Slowly, the price will start to go up.

As you can see, this is a cycle that will keep on going. You need to learn how to read these different parts of the cycle in order to help you to purchase the property at the right time and then sell it at the right time to earn as much money as possible. If you make a purchase of a home during the peak, then you are going to spend so much more money on the property and you will not be able to make any money in the process because it is unlikely the prices will go up higher.

Now, before you get into the market, it is important to figure out where in the market your current area is. If you notice that your area is at the tipping point, this is probably not a good time to make a purchase because prices are high and interested buyers are low. You won't make much of a profit off these properties. But if you notice that your area is at the bottom and there seems to be more confidence in the real estate market, you may want to make a purchase while the prices are low and deals are good. The hope here is that by the time you make some of the adjustments to the house and finish with closing, the market will be into more of a climb or in the peak, and you can profit even more from that.

While you can take some time to learn more about the market cycle and how it works, one of the best ways to recognize the signs of the market is to gain experience. You may find that it is hard to do this in the beginning, but as you work in the market and start to get involved with the investment, it will become so much easier to learn when you should enter and when you should sell.

While some investors will just go right out there and try to find a property in the beginning, the best investors are the ones who understand that the market is going to really determine if they are going to really get a discount on the home and even when they are able to sell the property when they are done. Learn the different parts of the market cycle and you are sure to get the best profit possible.

Chapter 3

How to Find Properties to Make You Money in Real Estate

There are a lot of things to consider when you are ready to get into the real estate market. You want to make sure that you are able to get the money to purchase a property, that you will be able to maintain that property while you own it, and decide whether you would like to flip that property or use it to make a rental income. When you are ready to get started in this market, you need to be able to pick out the right strategy that will help you make money. For example, you are going to need to do things differently if you want to flip a home compared to what you would do if you wanted to rent out the home. Let's take a look at some of the strategies that you can follow when it is time to purchase your first property in real estate.

Buy and hold strategy

So, the first strategy we are going to look at is known as the buy and hold strategy. This is one of the most common options that you can go with when you are ready to make money in real estate. For this strategy, you are going to find a property that is selling for a good price, and then you will make changes to it before renting it out to others to use. This is an easy form of investing because you may not have to do as much work with it and you can keep making the income year after year. People are going to be willing to pay you good rates for rent as long as you keep the property nice and you take care of them.

There are a lot of advantages that come with using the buy and hold investment strategy. One advantage is that you are able to make some income each month. As long as you were able to get the home for a good discount, you will be able to charge a rent that is high enough to cover the mortgage, the insurance, and anything else that you owe on the house. So, not only are you making a little bit of income in the process, but you are also able to pay down your mortgage and earn equity in the home at the same time. You can choose to use this equity to your advantage later on if you want to purchase more properties or if you would like to hold on to more of the profit if you sell the home later on.

Getting started with the buy and hold strategy is going to require a little bit of legwork. You can't go out and purchase the first home you see or you will end up with a mortgage that is too high for you to cover with rent prices. There are a lot of beginners who will go out and search for a home and who will then make some bad deals because they don't know which homes to look for or what price point they need to stick with. First, make sure you calculate how much you will have to spend on the home to make it livable. This will include the mortgage and the insurance on the home as well as how much money you need to put towards it to fix the property up. Then figure out how much rent you will need to charge to cover all this plus give you some profits. If this amount is not in line with the rent prices in your area, then the property is not a good investment.

You also need to make sure that you are willing to take the necessary steps to maintain the property. This means you are willing to fix things when they are broken, keep the property looking nice, and pick out tenants that are going to treat your property with respect along the way. There are a lot of decisions that go into picking out a property that works with the buy and hold strategy outside of just grabbing the first house that comes up on the market.

In order to make sure you are able to use this strategy successfully, you will need to learn about the market cycles that we discussed a little bit before. When you start to notice that the properties in your area are getting to a low point (or when the prices of these properties are low because there is a lot of available inventory), then this is the time when you would purchase a property for this strategy. Then, once you start to see that the market is beginning to go back up again, you will avoid making any purchases of these properties because their prices will be too high for you to earn money with this strategy.

Now, some people go into the buy and hold strategy because they want to hold on to them and have some rental properties. They have no plans to sell the properties at all; they just want to have these rental properties in their portfolio. This is a great way to make money, and it is still important for you to consider the market cycle to make it work. If you can purchase a property when the market is at a low point for prices, it will be much easier to find a good deal on a home and it is easier to offer competitive rent while still making a profit.

On the other hand, there are some investors who know that they need to get a good deal on a property in order to sell it for a good profit. The best time to purchase the property will be during one of those downturns in the market. But sometimes it can take a while before the market goes back up. This does not happen all the time and can result in a few years passing before the market goes up enough to make a profit on that home.

Instead of holding on to that property and paying the mortgage and taxes without any profit, these investors may consider temporarily renting out their homes. They can then make a profit on the rent, but then, when the market goes back up again, they can stop renting and instead sell the home. This is a great way to make sure you can earn as much on the properties while still getting a good deal on them.

Now, you can also choose to use this strategy while holding on to more than one property at a time. This will increase the amount of profit you will make each month because you will be able to combine the income from all the properties together. Most beginners are going to start with just one property, though, to help them learn the ropes and because that's probably all the money they have available. Once you get one property paid down and you have some equity available, you can consider bringing more properties into the mix to help you earn more money.

Flipping properties

Another popular option that you can choose for investing in real estate is known as property flipping. This is the type of real estate investment that you would see on some of those popular home improvement shows, but be aware that a lot of hard work goes into a house flip and you are not likely to make hundreds of thousands of dollars on each flip like they do on television. But, as an investor, if you are good at finding some deals on a home and you are ready to get your hands dirty, then this is a great way to make money in real estate.

The idea behind flipping properties is that you need to find a good property that has many features that a seller is looking for but there is something wrong with it that causes its worth and price to be lower than it should be. Sometimes the things that make the price of the property low are really simple fixes and you can quickly turn things around and make a large profit. Sometimes it may just be as simple as someone needing to get rid of the property quickly. You would find this good deal, purchase the property, do a few improvements, and then sell it to make a profit. Hopefully things would work out so that you would be able to sell the property for a comparable price to other homes in the area, so it would be easier for you to sell it as well.

Most investors who go into flipping homes will focus on a single family home since these are the easiest to use with this option. A good rule of thumb that you can use for flipping homes is the 70% rule. With this one, you will only purchase homes that are being sold for 70% of their current value, less any of the costs of rehab. For example, let's say that a home is worth $100,000 in its current area if it were sold in good condition, but you are going to have to put about $20,000 into it to make it look nice. According to the rule of 70%, you would not purchase this home for more than $50,000 to make a good profit. You could then make the adjustments to the home and then sell it for that $100,000 when you are done. Remember this is just something to consider and picking out the home that you will use, while also considering the costs, will vary depending on each unique situation.

When you are flipping homes and you want to make some good money, you need to learn how to be fast. The longer you have the property after you make the purchase the more money you end up spending on that property in the form of insurance, taxes and a mortgage. And then you need to add to this the costs of fixing up the home. When figuring out how much money you need to flip the home, remember that you need to calculate all the things above for at least a few months. It will take some time to make the fixes you want, and most homes will sit on the market for a few months before they sell.

When doing your calculations, you can consider using the property as a rental. This is a good idea if you are worried about the market staying at the low point for some time but you don't want to miss out on a good deal on a property. But as soon as you purchase the property, start advertising that it is for rent, even while you are fixing it up. It takes some time to find interested renters and you need to screen them all before you let them onto the property.

There is a lot of work that comes with the job of flipping homes and you must be an active participant in it all. You need to find a good deal on a property, find the right funding, and fix up the property as quickly as possible so you can get it listed on the market again as soon as possible.

Wholesaling

This is an option that can make you some good money in real estate, but it is not one that a lot of investors know about. With this particular strategy, you are going to work to find some good deals on a property, write out a contract that lets you have that deal, and then you will be able to sell that contract to another investor or someone else who is interested in that property. In most cases, the wholesaler is never technically going to own the property, just the contract. Instead, they are in charge of looking around for some good properties and then will get them set up for another person to make the purchase. The investor or other person who ends up purchasing the contract will pay the amount of the contract along with a fee for the work the wholesaler does.

There are many ways in which the wholesaler will be able to sell off these contracts. Sometimes they will be able to sell their contracts to some retail buyers, but often these contracts will go to some investors, such as other house flippers, who are known to be cash buyers. When dealing with a cash buyer, the wholesaler will get the benefit of not having to wait for the bank to close on a deal, saving a lot of time and hassle.

Many investors like working as a wholesaler because it is known to be one of the easiest investment options in the real estate market. You will not need to worry about as many upfront costs and the wholesaler doesn't technically own the property at any time, so they won't have to worry about the costs of fixing up the property, loan fees, contractors, tenants, and banks. The potential profit is not as high as house flipping or a good rental property, but there is less risk and if you are good at finding discount properties, it can help you to make some good money.

While there are a lot of good benefits to working with wholesaling, there is some work and a few risks with choosing this option. The wholesaler must always be on the lookout for a good deal so that they have inventory ready to sell to their contacts. They need to also have a good funnel for marketing so that they can attract the right leads during this time. And once you have a property contract, you must be able to find buyers who actually want the property as well or you will end up owning the property yourself.

Wholesaling is often touted as a method of investing in real estate that doesn't need any money. While you are able to work on the contracts and sell them without having to use any money, you do need to have some financial resources in order to create the marketing funnel to reach both the sellers and the buyers. But if you are successful at finding the right marketing tunnel for your needs and you can provide some good deals to investors, you can make a great income from this option without spending a lot of money on startup costs.

Chapter 4

How to Finance Your Investment

If you have ever taken a look at the home prices in your area, you know that it is going to take some serious capital to get started with investing in real estate. Most homes are going to cost over $100,000, even at a discount. And then you will need to fix up many of them before you are able to sell them or rent them out. Now, you will not necessarily need to have all that money on hand to get started. You can take out a mortgage from the bank, but this can take some time to work with and you will be responsible for bank fees and for interest until you are able to sell the property.

Since most people do not have enough money on them or saved up to finance the purchase of a property, there are a few financing options that the investor is able to choose from to get started. These are going to make it easier to get some of the money that you need to purchase the property as well as providing you with funds to make some improvements to the property as well. However, you must make sure that you are prepared before you ask for funding.

Banks, portfolio lenders, and some other options are willing to provide you with some funds, but they want to make sure that they will be able to get their investment back. You need to have your finances in order, a good business plan in place, a good credit score, and even a marketing plan before you even go to talk to some of these groups.

The good news is the first property is going to be the hardest to fund. You will have to prove that you will be a good person for this investment without any proof. After you have done this a few times, the banks and lenders will be able to tell that you know what you are doing, and you will have some cash behind you to use as well, so it becomes easier to keep on going.

But if you are a beginner who doesn't have a ton of capital to work with, it is important to search for a good lender who is willing to give you a chance and will give you the funds you need at a good rate. Some of the different funding options you can go with include:

Conventional mortgage

The first option that you may want to go with is known as a conventional mortgage. This is a good one to go with because it allows you to get started with a certain percentage down. The regular conventional loan will ask for twenty percent down on the property, but there are some other options you can pursue that will allow you to start with a lower down payment. The conventional mortgage can take more work, but they often provide the lowest interest rates and the best terms to work with.

When you are looking into a conventional mortgage, you are going to be responsible for doing much of the legwork. You must provide them with a lot of information about yourself to help them determine if you will be able to pay the mortgage back. You should prove your income history, your assets, that you have a good credit score, and that you are able to handle all your current debts while holding on to the new mortgage. Depending on the bank you go to, there may be some additional information that they will require from you, but start by filling out an application and go from there with the bank.

To help increase your chances of getting the funding you need, it is best to go with a bank that you already do business with, or at least one that is local to your area. This helps because they often want to help out new businesses in their area and they may already have some of the required information about you that they need.

203K loans

This is another option you can go with and it is part of the popular FHA loans. It will allow you as the investor to purchase a new property that needs some work. It not only allows you to get funds to purchase the home, but it provides you with some funds to help repair the home as well. All of these will be wrapped up into one loan, rather than having to take out several at the same time, so you will only have one payment to worry about.

Hard money

You can also choose to go with a financing option that is known as hard money. With this option, you will get financing from private businesses and individuals who know that you plan to invest in real estate with that money. There are some different terms that you can use with this kind of funding, but you and the other party will be able to come up with the specifics between yourselves. Some of the common terms and conditions that come with this kind of funding include:

- The loan you receive must be based on the value of the property and how much it is worth.
- These loans are usually not long-term loans. You will be expected to pay them back within 6 months to 3 years.
- The rate of interest you will pay on these loans will be much higher than traditional loans.
- There is going to be a high loan point on these loans. What this means is you will need to pay a lot of fees on these loans.
- Most lenders who are giving out this money will need you to verify what income you make.
- You will find that most lenders for this are not going to take the time to pull up your credit

score and this transaction is not going to show up on your credit report.
- These loans can be funded quickly, which can be nice if you want to jump on a deal quickly.
- Most of the time the lenders have the understanding that you will need to do a bit of work on the property before they can earn their money back.

If you want to flip a home and you would like to make sure that you can get the money quickly, you will find that working with a hard money loan is a great option for you. But you need to get the work on the home done quickly and sell the home fast because the terms of these loans are not going to last long.

Private money

You can also choose to work with private money. This kind of funding is slightly different than working with hard money lending. This is because hard lenders are professional investors and they expect you to follow the terms directly for the investment. With a private money lender, there is more flexibility. These lenders are just getting into the market and want you to do the work in real estate while they make the profit. In some cases, you and the private lender can have a close relationship as well.

Partnerships

Depending on your credit score and your finances, it may be hard for you to find the funding you need to get into real estate all on your own. You may not make enough income, have too much debt or not enough money to put in as a down payment and so the bank refuses your application. If this is the case for you, it may be worth your time to consider getting into a partnership with someone else who wants to enter real estate investing to increase your chances of getting funding.

You will find that the bank will look more favorably on your request for funding when you are in a partnership. This is because they now have the ability to hold two people responsible for paying that money back, and they are more likely to get at least some of the money back. The bank will be able to count the income from both individuals and this makes the debt to income ratio easier to manage. Of course, when you work in a partnership, you will need to share the profits, but it can certainly help when you have to share in the work.

Before you decide to go with a partnership, you must make sure that you are picking the right person to go into this partnership with. You need someone with a good credit history, someone who has a good income, and someone who is actually going to be there to help you with the work. Picking someone who is missing some of these things can make it hard to get the funding you need and may leave you doing most of the work on the property while still sharing the profits.

While the ideal situation is to use all of your own money to make the purchases because this can be the easiest, it costs the least amount because you won't have to pay interest or other fees, and you can keep all of the profit. But purchasing a home can be expensive and many real estate investors don't have that kind of money set aside to get started. Using one of these other forms of investing can make it easier to get the money you need so you can purchase your home, rent it out or flip it, and start making money in real estate.

Chapter 5

How to Purchase Your First Property in Real Estate

At this point, you have probably taken some time to look at the market in your area and even talked to a few sources for funding and gotten that in place as well. Now that this is all organized, it is time to start taking the necessary steps in order to purchase your first property. There are some specific steps that you should take to ensure that you get a property at a good price, with little work required on it, so that you can get everything done and still make a good profit in the process. When you have decided that it is time to purchase that very first investment property, make sure that you are going through the following steps:

- First, you must pick out the strategy you would like to use. This is going to make it easier to determine which properties you would like to purchase. Rental properties versus flipping properties will have different requirements.
- You should also define what your selection criteria are. What exactly do you want to find in your property? Would you like this property to be in a certain location? What is the price you want to stick with? Do you want to rent out to a family or an individual? How much work are you able to put into the property after

you make the purchase? Having this information figured out ahead of time will help you to pick the right property without having to worry about getting distracted during your search.

- Pick out the financing you want to use. Since most people are not going to have the full amount of a property saved up when they purchase in real estate, you will often need to rely on a bank or another source for your funding. You can take the time while you are searching, but before you put in an offer, to get pre-approved for your loan.
- Look through online sites, the MLS, yard signs, classifieds, and even direct mail in order to see which properties are currently for sale in your area. You can do this on your own, although some individuals choose to work with a realtor to help them find the property they want. With each property you see, you must run it through the criteria you set in the earlier steps to make sure it is the right property for your needs. It is always a good idea to allow for a bit of wiggle room in case there is a property that is really good but slightly out of your criteria, but stick as close to them as possible.
- Make an offer. You can work with a realtor on this one. This is a good idea as a beginner purchasing your first home. The seller is going to be the one who pays the realtor, so it will not cost you anything at this point. Realtors

are trained to handle all the legal stuff of the house selling process, so they can be a good resource. There are some strategies you can use when purchasing a home and it depends on how much the seller wants for the property and how much you are able to pay. You should start out with a little bit of wiggle room here because the seller is likely going to want to negotiate on the price. Starting out at your maximum pretty much means that you are going to lose out.

- Negotiate. The seller is going to want to do some back and forth with you to get the best price they can. You should start out at an offer that is below what you are willing to spend so that the seller can negotiate with you. If the seller takes the first offer, you got a really good offer. If they counter, then you have some room to come back. When the seller takes your offer, the realtor will be able to help you write out the purchase agreement. If you are doing this on your own, you can print out a purchase agreement on your own as well.
- While you are waiting for the funding to come through, and after the seller has agreed to your offer, you must make sure that you go through and do all the proper inspections. This can give you a good idea of what issues are already present and need to be fixed on the property. Depending on the issue and the agreement between you and the seller, you may even be able to get the seller to handle some of the

repairs, which will save you time and money. If you skip these inspections, you are the one who will be on the hook for getting them all fixed on your own. Assume that the person you will sell the house to will do inspections, so, by doing one now, you can avoid some issues in the future inspection.

- During this time, you should also start talking to contractors who can help you get the work done. As soon as the loan and funding come through, the clock will start ticking. The longer you hold on to the property the more it is going to cost you as you make mortgage payments and more. You want to try to get quotes for how much it will cost to do the work and then see if you can get the contractors into the home as soon as possible after the closing. If you plan it all out, it may be possible to get the work done on the property within a few weeks, so you can relist it, or start renting it out, very quickly.
- Once you have completed all the inspections and you are happy with how they were handled, it is time to go to the Title and Escrow office to sign all the papers that are needed. Then the paperwork is going to be recorded and you are technically the owner of the home. You can start to get the home ready, get the contractors in, and start planning for how you will make a profit on the home. If you are going to rent it out, you can start listing the property for new tenants. If you plan to

sell it, get the work done quickly so that you can list it and get it sold. All of this needs to be done as quickly as possible.

One thing to remember is that you are usually given a little bit of a reprieve before your first payment is due. You can usually make it about two months before you need to send in the first payment. Depending on your agreement with the bank, you may be able to pay a little extra in interest at closing and get the payment period extended a little bit longer. Use this to your advantage to get the work done quickly without having to make payments on the home and hopefully save money in the process.

The process is going to work pretty similar to this when talking about residential or commercial real estate as well. You must always make sure that you are getting a good deal on the property that you pick, and it is important to do inspections to make sure that nothing is hidden in the property that could make you lose money. But if you follow your criteria and work with the right people who can take care of all the legal stuff, you will soon own a real estate investment and can decide what you would like to do with it to turn it into a money maker.

Chapter 6

How Brokers and Property Managers Can Make Your Job Easier

As someone who has just gotten started in real estate, you may want to consider working with some experts in the field to help you get going. There are many people you will need to work with in order to help you to purchase the property, rent the property, sell the property, fix up the property, and so much more. While it may make things easier if you were able to do it all on your own, this is just not something you will be able to do when you get into real estate. Working with property managers and real estate brokers can make your life so much easier and can help you to earn a lot of profit in this industry. Let's learn more about both groups of people to see how they will be able to help your real estate investment.

The real estate broker

The first person you will want to consider working with is a real estate broker. When it is time to buy or sell a property, it is often a good idea to work with a real estate broker. There are a lot of benefits to working with one of these brokers and, while you do need to pay them for their work, it actually will make it easier to come out ahead on your investment.

First, you can use a broker when you are ready to purchase a new property. Your real estate broker is often the first person an investor will call in order to help them find the property they want to use. These brokers know the area that you want to purchase in and are able to give some great insights about the prices in that area and where they will go in the near future. They also have all the connections that you need around town to find those great deals. These brokers seem to know everyone in the town and can get you to those deals long before anyone else can. You can try to do this all on your own, but you will find that it is much easier to work with a real estate broker.

Once you have found the property you would like to purchase, your broker will still be able to help you out. They are good at handling all the legal paperwork that is needed when it is time to put in an offer and do some negotiations along the way until a price is agreed upon. The broker will help you to walk through all this paperwork and can even point you to some suggestions about doing the inspections, and who to hire as a contractor, and can basically ensure that you are able to get into the new property as soon as possible.

After you purchase the new property and fix it up, or even after you have rented it out for some time and are finally ready to sell it after a few years, it is time to get the property ready to sell. You will be amazed at the difference a real estate broker can make when it comes to selling the home. There are some investors who try to save money and sell the house on their own, but real estate brokers are more efficient at getting property sold and are well worth the money.

When you are ready to go find a broker to work with on this adventure, you need to find one who is not only qualified to do the job but also one you can get along with. Real estate investing is something you can stick with for a long time and working with the same real estate broker can make the process easier. It can be nice to work with the same person throughout it all rather than having to restart the process with a new agent each time you want to purchase or sell a property.

Working with a property manager on your rentals

Rental properties are a great way to make money over the long term, especially if you are able to get a good deal on a property and you can pay down some of the mortgage. As you accumulate more rental properties, you are able to make more money in the process. Over time, you may decide that it is too much work for you to do all the stuff for each rental property such as collecting the rent, cleaning the homes, looking for new tenants and more. This is when you may want to consider hiring a property manager.

These property managers can help you to take care of all your rental properties so that you can concentrate on doing other things. They know how to run these rental properties and will make sure that you get your money out of each one. Yes, it does mean you will have to share some of your profits with them, but it also means you will not have to put in as much work on the properties.

When you are ready to pick out a good property manager to work with, some of the things to look for include:

- The first thing you should look at is how many properties that manager is in charge of. You want to make sure that they are not taking on too many other properties or they may run into trouble having time to manage yours as well. If a property manager seems to have a large number of properties they are in charge of, it is best to go with someone else.
- How much the manager charges. You also want to make sure that you are getting a good deal with a property manager who will not overcharge you. Most property managers will ask for seven to ten percent of your rental revenue on the properties they will look over. If you are talking to a manager who is asking for a number that is way off from this, then it is best to avoid them.
- What software the manager decides to use. A property manager is able to use different software programs to keep track of their costs and to collect the rent. You can check out the software and see if it will actually be able to do its job.

- Ask if the manager does inspections. You want to pick out a property manager who is willing to do routine inspections of your properties. You also want to make sure that they are not charging a lot of extra fees in order to do these inspections. And when the manager does the inspections, make sure they know the rules and know that they still need to be respectful of your current tenant, such as giving a good amount of notice so the tenant can be prepared. If you find that a manager is making it difficult for you to do a routine inspection to make sure that your properties are doing well, then it is a good idea to find a new manager.
- You should also make sure that you pick out a property manager you can get along with. There are some property managers who assume they know best and will try to take over control from you. If they won't listen to the way you want to do things, no matter what their experience is, or one of them talks over you, is hard to get ahold of or there is another issue, then there are plenty of other managers you can go with.

While it will eat into your profits a little bit, hiring a good property manager can make all the difference when it comes to taking care of your rental properties. As you grow your portfolio and you get more properties, it can be nice to have someone else who can take care of things so you can concentrate on growing your investment even more.

Chapter 7

Protecting Your Assets

When you decide to invest in real estate, you must understand that you are working on a new business. You may be ready to get the funding and start looking for the properties you want to use to start the investment, but you may not have thought about your investment as the business that it is. If you don't treat this new investment like one of your assets, you are running the potential for some trouble. Say that someone gets harmed on the property, whether it is a contractor or one of your tenants, you will be the one held liable for the injuries and damages. Depending on what kind of business you consider yourself to have you may have to worry about how much the other person could claim against you. Let's take a look at the most common types of businesses and how each one will handle your business.

Sole proprietor

If you go into this investment and you do not pick out an entity for your business, you will automatically be considered a sole proprietor. This is basically an individual who runs their business and who is going to be responsible for all parts of the business. You will probably call the business something with your own name and there isn't going to be a separation of your assets and your liabilities. Some people prefer this because it can help them to keep things simple and there won't be a lot of paperwork that you need to concentrate on. However, if there is some reason for someone to come after your business, then they can also come after some of your personal assets as well.

Limited liability company

This is another option you can choose to go with and it is considered a hybrid between a partnership and a corporation. Members who choose this entity for their business are going to have the flexibility and income benefits that come from being in a partnership or a sole proprietorship, without all the paperwork to deal with like working with a corporation. They will also get the benefit of limiting how much they are liable for if something goes wrong. There are a few legal differences between this and some of the others, so you will need to learn more about these, but this is a good option if you would like to protect some of your personal assets while still getting a lot of freedom in running your business.

Corporation

When you are working with a real estate investment, it is not likely that you will choose to work as a corporation, at least in the beginning. This is because a corporation is a large legal entity that will have to spend a lot of time on paperwork and all the formal stuff in order to get started. You will start with filing articles of incorporation inside your state and then you may have to consider working with stockholders. This can take away some of the freedom of making decisions. There are some benefits to using this kind of entity in your business, such as getting tax deductions to save you money. You do need to be a little bit careful about double taxation. This can occur when you get taxed on your profits and on the stockholder dividends.

S-corporation

This is a good option to go with if you would like to end up with some of the benefits that a corporation gets but you would like to be a small business rather than a large corporation. These are ones that are looking to get some of the tax advantages, as long as they are able to meet the requirements of the IRS. They can wave the corporate taxes and the owners of the company are able to report the income on their personal returns, helping them to avoid issues with being taxed more than once.

Which one should I pick?

For the most part, you will not want to work with a corporation because this is for bigger entities and the double taxation is going to cost you a lot of money, but while the sole proprietor option may seem tempting, you won't want to go with this either because it limits the amount of protection that you are going to get.

For real estate investing, most investors choose to go with the LLC option. This gives them the right mix between the sole proprietorship and the corporation. You will be able to be in control of this form of business entity and you won't have to listen to the views of stockholders to get things done, but you still get the protection of your personal assets with this structure. If you do decide to become a corporation, most of the time it is best to register as an s-corporation because it will save you money from the double taxation that occurs with normal corporations.

As you can see, there are a lot of things to consider when it comes to picking out the entity that you would like to give to your business. Each one has its own benefits and negatives and it often depends on what you would like to do with your business and how much protection you would like to have if something goes wrong.

As a beginner, you may assume that it doesn't matter whether or not you set yourself up as a business entity at all, but there are a lot of things that could happen with one of your properties. What if you hire a contractor who falls or gets hurt on the property or something happens with one of your tenants while they are living in the building? Without the right business entity in place, the individual in question could come after not only your business assets but also your personal assets. But with the help of a good business entity in place, you can protect yourself and deal more with the tasks of running your investment.

Chapter 8

How to Handle Your Lease When Renting out Properties

So far, we have spent some time talking about what you need to do if you are interested in purchasing a home and flipping it for a profit. But what happens if you would like to get a property and use it as a rental? Picking out the lease that you will use with your tenants is an integral part of helping you to keep your properties in good shape, keeping yourself protected, and ensuring that you pick out good tenants. These leases are meant to help protect both you and the tenant and they ensure that both parties know what is expected of them from the beginning. Some of the different types of leases that you can consider for your properties include:

Residential property leases

The first type of lease we are going to take a look at is a residential property lease and this is going to be different from what you would offer to a tenant of a commercial property. Sometimes these leases will change depending on what property you are working with. For example, when you work with a single-family home, you can consider having the tenant pay their own utilities in addition to the rent, while some landlords will lump the utilities into the rent for those living in apartments to make it easier. You can also consider whether you want to write out a short-term or a long-term lease.

The short-tern leases are going to be the ones that are for one year at a time. You can also offer ones that go for a shorter amount of time, like six months. There are even some apartments that are temporary living spaces for those who just need a place for a few months. You will have to spend more time getting tenants to fill the space, but you can also charge a lot more per month for these places than you could if someone stayed for a year or more.

You can also choose to write out leases that are long term. Most people will stick with leases that last one year at a time. Even if they end up staying for longer, they like that flexibility to move out if they would like. But there are others who are willing to stay in the property for two years or more in exchange for receiving a discount on their rent. This provides you with a guarantee of a steady income for two or three years and the tenant will be able to get a discount on what they are paying.

When you are picking out which lease is going to meet your needs the best, you need to consider all of the things you are going to cover. It is common for those who go into a single-family home to find that they need to pay for their own utilities and water and then the landlord would be responsible for things like maintaining the home and paying any taxes. If you are renting out larger complexes, you may find that it is easier to group the utilities together and then add that price to the rental price and the tenants will appreciate having it all combined as well. You should decide which extras, including ones that are not listed above, you are willing to provide to the tenant ahead of time.

Also, the lease needs to list out all of the responsibilities of the tenant. The tenant should be responsible for submitting their rent on time or the landlord will get the right to begin the eviction process. The tenant is also responsible for taking care of the property while they are living inside it and not allowing more than normal wear and tear inside the property. If the tenant does not uphold their rights in the rental agreement, the landlord will have some legal recourse that they can use.

The landlord is also going to have some responsibilities that they need to come up with. For example, if something goes wrong with the property, such as the water not working, the electricity or heat stopping or something similar, then the landlord is responsible for taking care of these right away. Just as the landlord has some legal recourse if the tenant doesn't pay or follow the lease properly, the tenant will have some legal recourse if the landlord does not keep the home properly taken care of.

Commercial property leases

In addition to working with single-family homes and apartments, you can work with commercial properties. These are going to work with slightly different rules that come with the commercial property leases, but this is because you are working with different types of tenants in the process. The terms will depend on what kind of property you are working with, how much the tenants make, and more. Let's take a look at some of the options that you can pick from when it comes to commercial property leases.

Full service lease

The first option you can go with is a full-service lease, which is one that is going to include everything in the rent. The landlord will pay everything on the property for the tenant including the maintenance, insurance, taxes, utilities, janitorial services and more. Before setting the rent, the landlord needs to go through and figure out how much all of that stuff would cost and then they can split it up between how many tenants they will have inside of the building. The landlord can even add in something to the lease that will protect them if one of the tenants uses up too much in utilities.

The rent for one of these will usually be higher because so much is included in the price. But some tenants like this because they can just pay one thing to take care of all their business needs. It keeps things easier, so they are willing to pay a bit more on their rent.

Net lease

Another option you are able to choose when working with commercial property leases is known as a net lease. With a net lease, you are going to charge the tenant a lower lease, and it will include the rental space for the business to use as well as usual costs like maintenance. The tenant will pay this inside of the lease and then the landlord will take care of these costs for the tenant. There are a few options that can fit into this type of lease as well:

- Single net lease: With the single net lease, the tenant will get the benefit of paying the lower base rent, but then they will need to do a prorated share of the property tax. This tax is something that all of the tenants will share in based on how much room they are going to take up inside of the building. The landlord will be able to pay for some of the expenses of using the building, but the individual tenants are responsible for some things like utilities and janitorial staff.
- Double net lease: This type of lease is where the tenant is going to be responsible for the base rent that the landlord charges, and then they will need to pay for their part of the property taxes and the insurance. The landlord

will still be in charge of paying for all the maintenance requirements of the building, but the tenant will need to pay for the utilities that they use.

- Triple net lease: As a landlord, you may be interested in going with the triple net lease on your commercial properties. With this type of lease, your tenant is going to be in charge of the base rent that you charge each month as well as their property taxes, utilities, common area utilities, janitorial services, insurance, and anything extra they would like to have in their building. This one is going to favor the landlord more than anything because the tenant is basically going to pay for everything, but the tenant may like this because it allows them to be more transparent to their customers.

There are many options that come with picking out a lease with commercial properties and working out the best option that will attract the right companies into the area while still making a good profit. Carefully consider each of these options before deciding to ensure you get the best option for both you and your tenant.

Chapter 9

How to Avoid Common Mistakes

As a beginner, you are trying to get used to the whole idea of working in real estate. You want to be able to earn money back on your investment as soon as possible and you do not want to end up failing in the process. Learn some of the common mistakes that beginners make and how to avoid them. Follow some of the tips below, and you are sure to make a good return on investment in the real estate market in no time.

Forgetting the marketing plan

Real estate investing is just like a business and you need to treat it as such if you want to see success. A marketing plan can help to bring the different parts of the business together and it can really help you to define your goals and your timeline for achieving some of these goals. First, when you approach the bank to get some of the funding that you need, you will be required not only to have information on your income and credit history, but they will also want to see your marketing or business plan to determine whether you are ready.

While a marketing plan may seem like it takes up a lot of time and isn't really necessarily, if you want to see success, you need to have this business plan in place. Consistently, beginners and professionals who have this marketing plan (and who have it all written out) are more likely to find success compared to those who never make one of these plans.

Starting a business or marketing plan can be tough and you may not know where to start. There are several business plans available online that you can use for your needs. Just go online and find the one you like the best and then fill in the blanks to make it relevant for your real estate business.

Not using your available resources

There are actually a lot of different resources available for those who are trying to get into the real estate market. You can work with a real estate agent who will be able to answer your questions and help you to find the right properties or help you sell your property. There are contractors who can help you to get the work done in no time. There are bankers who can point out the best options for loans and resources to make your investments better than before.

As a beginner, there is nothing wrong with using all the resources provided to you. Some of the best investors in the market are using these resources so it makes sense that you should be using them as well. Find the ones that will help out with your particular investing method and stick with them.

The bidding war

It is important that you never go into an investment and get into a bidding war with other interested buyers over the same property. It may be one of the best properties out there, but as soon as you get into a bidding war with others, the discount price that you were going for on that property will go out the window. You can easily get into the mindset that you must have this property and that you can't let someone else have it. And that will play on your emotions, rather than on your logic, and can make it hard to make money in the long term.

If you get into a bidding war and find that others are going for the same property, it is probably best to just let the property go. Otherwise, if the emotions start going and you get stuck in a loop of not wanting to let it go, you are going to end up paying a lot more for the property than you can afford or even more than the property is worth. Remember that bidding wars are great for the seller because they increase the amount they will be able to earn on the home, but they can be a pain for investors who want to get the house for a low price.

Purchasing a home and not seeing it before

It is never a good idea to purchase a home that you have not been able to personally look over yourself. It doesn't matter how good of a deal that property is. It does not matter how the market is doing. It does not matter how much you trust the person who tells you about the property. This is your investment and you need to be active in determining whether this is the right investment for you by seeing that property before purchasing.

Pictures and virtual tours never work out well if you don't see the property. They are great for the buyer to get a good idea of the layout of the building and to make some decisions about whether this property is even something they are interested in, but the house is going to look much different than the pictures the seller presents. Of course, the seller is going to post pictures that show the home in the best light possible. But when you get to the home, you may notice that the rooms appear smaller, the garage is in a weird location on the property, the neighbor has some loud dogs that bark all day long or other issues that will affect how well you will be able to sell the property or rent it out later on. Always go and see the property in person before you get too attached or decide to purchase the home.

Not understanding your budget

You have to set a budget right from the beginning and learn how to stick with it as closely as possible. And you need to remember all of the things that you need to include in the budget. It is easy to think that it is only going to take you a month or two to get the home ready to sell, but what happens if it takes you six months or longer to sell the home? And did you really calculate all of the costs, not just the mortgage but also the taxes and insurance on the property? And how much is it going to cost to repair the home before you can sell it, and did you leave some cushion room in case things are not going the way you would like them to?

As you can see, things can start to get out of control if you are not careful with your budget. If you purchase the home for more than your budget, you may not be able to recover it later on. If your contractors are not able to stick with your budget or your timeline, it could ruin your budget as well. If it takes longer to sell the home, you may pay more than you had planned.

Come up with a budget and stick to it or leave a little bit of breathing room in case things do not go the way you want. If you are someone who struggles with budgeting in your regular life, it may not be a good idea to get into budgeting when you are dealing with real estate.

Getting into kitchen and bathroom remodels

It is really tempting to get into a new property and think you need to remodel the kitchen and the bathroom. This can be an issue because maybe one or both of these rooms look horrible inside the home and you know that you will never be able to sell the property if you do not make some changes. The biggest issue here is that these kinds of remodels are really expensive and do not give you the return on investment you wish. If you spend $20,000 on remodeling one of these rooms, it may make the house look better, but you would be lucky if it raised the price of the home more than a few thousand dollars.

There are a few things that you can do here. If the kitchen and bathroom need just a few little things to make them look better, such as a quick paint job or taking carpet out of them and adding some tile, then it is worth your time to go for the house (as long as the rest of the repairs are not too extensive) and pay a bit for them. This will help you to sell the house, and if the repairs are small, then you can easily make the money back.

However, if you are looking at these rooms and you feel that you need to replace a lot of things inside of the home, from the flooring to the sinks and counters and everything else, then it is probably best to go with a different house. Many times, you will not be able to sell the home without fixing them, and it is best to let someone else take on the headache.

Working in real estate is something that can take a lot of time and effort in order to see some success. It can provide you with a good profit when you are done, but many new investors do not realize how much time, money, and work they will need to put in to see these profits. Make sure you take a look at some of these common mistakes and figure out how you can avoid them to make the most profit.

Conclusion

Thank you for making it through to the end of this book, let's hope it was informative and able to provide you with all of the tools you need to achieve your goals, whatever they may be.

The next step is to decide what kind of real estate investing you would like to do. There are so many options available to you and to others who would like to get started, but it does take some time and some work. This guidebook took a look at all the different aspects of investing in real estate and what you need to do to get started. From picking out a good property to finding the funding you need to see success, working with a real estate agent, protecting your assets, and setting up leases if you decide to go with rental properties, you are sure to learn everything you need to know in order to get started in real estate investing today!

Finally, if you found this book useful in anyway, a review on Amazon is always appreciated!

Real Estate Investing

*The Advanced Guide to Real Estate Investing
(Learn the Secret Hints and Tips to Make Money Learn the Secret Hints and Tips to Make Money in Today's Market)*

© Copyright 2018 by John James

All rights reserved.

The following eBook is reproduced below with the goal of providing information that is as accurate and reliable as possible. Regardless, purchasing this eBook can be seen as consent to the fact that both the publisher and the author of this book are in no way experts on the topics discussed within and that any recommendations or suggestions that are made herein are for entertainment purposes only. Professionals should be consulted as needed prior to undertaking any of the action endorsed herein.

This declaration is deemed fair and valid by both the American Bar Association and the Committee of Publishers Association and is legally binding throughout the United States.

Furthermore, the transmission, duplication or reproduction of any of the following work including specific information will be considered an illegal act irrespective of whether it is done electronically or in print. This extends to creating a secondary or tertiary copy of the work or a recorded copy and is only allowed with express written consent from the Publisher. All additional rights reserved.

The information in the following pages is broadly considered to be a truthful and accurate account of facts and, as such, any inattention, use or misuse of the information in question by the reader will render any resulting actions solely under their purview. There are no scenarios in which the publisher or the original author of this work can be in any fashion deemed liable for any hardship or damages that may befall them after undertaking information described herein.

Additionally, the information in the following pages is intended only for informational purposes and should thus be thought of as universal. As befitting its nature, it is presented without assurance regarding its prolonged validity or interim quality. Trademarks that are mentioned are done without written consent and can in no way be considered an endorsement from the trademark holder.

Introduction

Congratulations on downloading this book and thank you for doing so.

The following chapters will discuss how you can invest your money and put it to work for you to create a better future for you and your family.

Are you like most of us, tired of your day job and wishing that something better would come along? Are you struggling every month to make ends meet and wondering what you can do to help yourself? Are you just in need of some passive income for retirement? Do you have extra money in the bank that you wish would earn higher returns than the bank pays?

If you answered yes to any of these questions, then this book is for you. This book will tell you how you can get involved in real estate at any level of investment and spend only as much time as you want to spend on it.

You will learn all the secrets the banks don't want you to know about how you can get approved for the loans you need so that you can get started investing in real estate with little to no upfront money.

You will learn how to make sure that your personal assets are protected in an uncertain world so that you can enjoy peace of mind, even if the worst happens.

You will learn all you need to know about the different kinds of real estate investments that are out there, as well as the risks and rewards for each, so that you can make the best decision for you and your family. You will also learn what level of personal involvement is required by each so that you can find the perfect match for your level of interest in real estate.

Whether your interest in real estate investment is purely casual or you are thinking of making it a second career, this book will be your ultimate guide to get started.

There are plenty of books on this subject on the market, thanks again for choosing this one! Every effort was made to ensure it is full of as much useful information as possible. Please enjoy!

Chapter 1

Real Estate vs. the Stock Market

Prior to the start of the Industrial Revolution, wealth was mostly measured in precious metals like gold and silver, livestock like cattle and sheep, and land. If you wanted to invest your money, those were your main options. During the Industrial Revolution, large companies came to be publicly owned and traded. Shares of ownership of these companies are called stock and are bought and sold on stock markets. This introduced a new way for those with extra money to invest it and make it grow.

So, you have some extra money, and you are looking for the best way to invest it. People frequently wonder which is better in today's world—real estate or the stock market. Unfortunately, there is no easy answer to this. Is a Mercedes Benz better than a BMW? Is prime rib better than veal? It's simply a matter of preference. It also comes down to the specifics of each individual investment. There are no universal rules in investing your money; you must carefully examine each opportunity and decide for yourself whether it is right for you. After all, this is *your* hard-earned money, and nobody will protect it better than you.

Neither real estate nor the stock market is better than the other. They are simply different. But that is not to say that the choice between the two doesn't matter;

each investor must decide for himself which option best matches their short-term and long-term investment strategy.

If you had been in a position to buy up a bunch of beachfront property in the 1960s and 1970s prior to the California real estate explosion, very few stocks could compete with the returns over a couple decades.

And what real estate on Earth could compete with the returns if you had invested in shares of Microsoft, Facebook or Walmart in the early days, especially if you just kept rolling over your dividends? So, the answer is not a one-size-fits-all. The most successful investors have a diverse portfolio that includes stock and real estate investments.

Let's dive in by taking a look at both kinds of investment:

Real Estate: When investing in real estate, all you are doing is buying a piece of physical land or property. Some real estate takes money out of your pocket every month that you own it—for example, a vacant lot that you will sell one day to a developer, but, in the meantime, you are still paying taxes, maintenance, etc. Some real estate brings money in— for example, an apartment building, rental houses or a commercial building where the occupants are sending you money each month. You use that money to pay any expenses, and the difference is your profit each month.

Stocks: When you buy shares of stock, you are buying part of a company. Whether that company makes TVs, cell phones or bread or sells cars or develops new apps, as one of the owners you get a share of any profit that company earns. The more stock you own the higher your share of the profit. The stock market may seem complicated, but it couldn't be easier. If a company has issued 10,000 stocks and you own 1,000 of them, you own 10% of that company. Therefore, every year the company pays out dividends, as a 10% owner of that company you will receive 10% of the payout. As a 10% owner, you will also have 10% of the say over how the company is to be run.

Real Estate vs. Stocks – Pros and Cons

Now we will discuss the pros and cons of each of these to give you a better understanding of which better matches your investing goals.

Real estate pros:

The average person usually finds real estate to be a more comfortable investment to get started. Children of the American working and middle classes often grow up hearing their parents emphasize the importance of home ownership, while upper-class children often hear discussions of the stock market during their formative years. The result is that the middle class is more likely to invest in real estate than they are in stocks or bonds.

When you invest in real estate, you're investing in something real and solid. You can drive up to it and see and touch it, you can take photos of it to show your friends, you have the feeling of pride of ownership. It's *yours*. Many investors find that important when looking into where to put their money because we work hard for our money and we want something to show for it. Because they only represent an *idea,* a share of ownership in a company, it may be hard for many to see any value in a stock certificate.

Borrowing money to invest in real estate can be much safer than borrowing money to buy stock (margin trading) due to the different ways the loans are structured.

Compared to stocks, it's much harder to be ripped off in real estate. If you do your homework and go examine the property itself, make your own repairs, vet your tenants yourself, you will not be taken by surprise. It's hard to hide deception in real estate; the property is either there and in the advertised condition or not. With stocks, you kind of just have to take everybody at their word and trust that the management of the company knows their business and that the auditors are on the ball. This can be unsettling for many investors.

Real estate investments are a great way to protect yourself against inflation in the long term. Inflation happens when the government puts new dollars into circulation, thereby watering down the value of the other dollars already in circulation. When that happens, the cost of almost all goods, including real estate, increases to offset the inflation. Plus, if it is a rental property the cost of rent will increase over time. It is not that these properties necessarily increase in value; you as the owner are simply raising the prices to occupy and use the property to offset the lower value of the dollar.

If one of your primary goals in investing is to protect your savings against the government's rampant printing of new money to service international debts, real estate may be ideal for you. As Mark Twain once said, "Buy land, they're not making it anymore!"

Real estate cons:

In comparison with stocks, real estate requires a lot of time. When you buy a stock, your work is pretty much done. You can simply put it into a safe deposit box and wait until the dividends, if any, come to you. As a real estate owner, you are on call 24/7 if something goes wrong with one of your units like a clogged toilet, gas leak or a fire, and you are liable to get sued if somebody is injured on your property. Even if you hire a property manager or are only involved in real estate as an investor, you will still have to attend meetings and otherwise invest time that stocks do not require.

As mentioned above, if one of your properties is unoccupied it will cost you money to own it. You will still have to pay Uncle Sam his taxes every month, as well as any maintenance costs, utilities, insurance, and countless other things you likely haven't thought of yet. So, if circumstances beyond your control cause a higher than expected vacancy rate in your units, you could easily lose money! At the end of the day, an empty building is worth nothing to you.

For the most part, real estate does not really increase in value after adjusting for inflation. As we discussed above, real estate is great protection against inflation, but the real value of real estate rarely increases faster than inflation. How does this work? Let's say you invest $20,000 of your own money in buying a $100,000 house, borrowing the other $80,000. With an inflation rate of only 3%, the house you bought for $100,000 is now worth $103,000, not because the real "value" increased but because it now takes 3% more dollars to purchase anything due to inflation. But you only invested $20,000, so that means you earned $3,000 from a $20,000 investment or a 15% return! Taking inflation into account, that is a 12% return before taking ownership expenses into account. This attractive return on investment is what makes real estate so intriguing.

Stock market pros:

Nearly all research has proven that buying stocks, reinvesting your profits into more stocks, and holding your stocks long term is the greatest creator of wealth yet invented, even accounting for all the crashes. No other asset brings money in like owning a business, and when you own stocks, you own part of a business. But, while running your own small business requires a large investment of your time, owning part of a business in the form of stocks only requires a little homework upfront to make sure the company is a good fit for you. Professional managers watched over by a board of directors run the company. You get the benefits of their work without having to show up at the offices every day. This is truly passive income.

If you had invested only $1,000 in Amazon when it went public in 1997 (remember, at that time it was only an online bookstore), you would now have over $480,000 worth of stock, and that's if you didn't roll your earnings back into the company! That's right—a return on investment of over 48,000 percent over only a couple of decades. On top of that, you would also have your yearly cash dividend payout coming in every year with no effort on your part.

It is much easier to diversify when investing in stocks than when investing in real estate. Some mutual funds only require you to invest as little as a hundred bucks a month, and some companies let you invest in dozens of different companies for a flat rate as low as only a few dollars a month. Even the smallest real estate investment requires much more than $100. Real estate usually represents a pretty significant investment for most folks.

In case you need cash quick, it is far easier to cash out of stocks than it is with real estate. During normal trading hours, you can sell your entire stock portfolio in a matter of moments if you wish to. Trying to sell a piece of real estate is a process that can take days, months or even years in some cases.

It is also a lot easier to borrow against stocks than real estate. You can simply write a check against your stock trading account once a broker has approved you for margin borrowing. (Margin borrowing is simply borrowing money against stocks that you already own to purchase more stocks in the expectation that the new stocks will increase in value more than the interest you will pay the lender.)

Stock market cons:

In spite of their proven long-term ability to create more wealth, most stock market investors are unable to benefit from this. This is because people, by nature, are fickle, undisciplined and prone to panic when it comes to investing. These folks actually end up losing money in the market because of fear and a sort of herd instinct. For example, during the most recent financial collapse in the late 2000s, many investors panicked and sold their shares at a time when the market had lost over half of its value—the exact wrong strategy. Disciplined investors buy when the market is at its lowest and everyone else is panicking.

The stock market can be volatile. Stock prices will soar and crash in the short term. Your $100 investment may go to $500 one day then to $50 the next. If you did your homework before buying that stock, this shouldn't concern you; you may even see this as a chance to double down when the stock is at its lowest and buy more or cash out part of your investment when it reaches its high point, if you think the stock is overvalued at that price.

When looking at growth charts, stocks seem like they have not really done anything for the past decade. They may seem stagnant and like a low-yield investment. But this is because growth charts don't take reinvested dividends into account. As mentioned above, every year a profitable company sends its shareholders a check for their percentage of the profits; this is the dividend check. The canny investor reinvests these dividends into the company by using them to purchase more stock so that his dividend checks get larger every year.

You now have a pretty good overview of the differences between the stock market and real estate investment. As mentioned, both are great investments, and your long-term goal should be to have a diverse portfolio that consists of both stocks and real estate.

But this book concerns real estate investment, so if you've made it this far and real estate investing still seems like a good fit for you, read on to discover how to get started.

For most people, real estate is the easiest investment to understand because there is an exchange of money for a tangible good. This is appealing because it is simple and straightforward. As long as the rent comes in every month from the tenant and the landlord keeps the water flowing and toilet flushing, everybody wins. However, investing in real estate can be more complicated than this. This is because there are several kinds of real estate investment, ranging from industrial to residential, and even some real estate that trades on stock exchanges. This book was written to help you wade through the options.

To put it as simply as possible, the goal when investing in real estate is to put your money to work for you at once so that it will grow into more money down the road. Your profit, or "return on investment" (ROI), must be enough to cover all of your ownership costs while still providing enough to make your risk worthwhile.

Investing in real estate can be as simple as playing Monopoly when you have a grasp of the basic factors of economics, investment, and risk.

To win, you buy properties, avoid bankruptcy, and generate rent so that you can buy more properties and start the cycle again. However, remember that simple is not the same as easy or without risk. If you lose at this game, the long-term consequences can be disastrous. You could even end up bankrupt.

There are several ways for you to make money from real estate. This is why it's such a great investment in the right market.

Incoming rent. This is, perhaps, the most common type of real estate investment. You invest in a property, such as an apartment building, and every month your tenants send you money in exchange for being allowed to occupy one of your units. But this does not just have to be residential properties; this can include office buildings, laundromats, storage units, restaurants, really anything that someone may want to lease from you for a certain period of time. This is probably the most time-consuming kind of real estate investment, but it can be an ongoing source of income.

Appreciation. Appreciation is when the value of your property increases due to a boom in the real estate market, your neighborhood suddenly becoming gentrified, a large popular business moving into the neighborhood, increasing commercial traffic, or you investing time and effort to make improvements to the property, making it more appealing to potential renters or buyers. Relying on appreciation for you to make a return on your investment can be difficult. It is often impossible to know which will be the next desirable neighborhood or how buyers will react to any change in the neighborhood or in the property itself. It can be quite profitable, but it is certainly not as safe as rental income.

Act as a middleman. In almost any real estate transaction, money doesn't just pass between buyer and seller. There are people who specialize in the real estate industry and make your life easier during the transaction in exchange for a percentage of the sale price, this can include real estate agents, who advertise your home and negotiate the sale for you. There are real estate brokers, who make a commission from each property that is sold, or property management companies, who will manage your rental properties for you in exchange for a percentage of the income. For example, the property management company earns a certain percentage of the tenants' rent payments in exchange for taking care of all the maintenance, fixing what needs to be fixed, keeping the grounds looking nice, finding good tenants, etc. A very fair deal, actually.

Miscellaneous Real Estate Income. If you own an apartment complex, perhaps you have a laundry room where tenants can safely wash their clothes near to their home in exchange for a few quarters. Maybe you have vending machines in your office buildings to provide snacks to the employees there. Arcade video games in the lobbies of restaurants. These are the kinds of other sources of real estate income that are often overlooked. Ways to get a return on investment from your properties are only limited by your imagination.

Hopefully, now you are excited about the potential that investing in real estate can hold. But to invest in real estate you need money, usually more money than you will have available. Fortunately, there are numerous lenders you can apply to for a loan. Our next chapter will focus on how to make yourself stand out when lenders are reviewing your loan application.

Chapter 2

Attracting Lenders

There are several ways to make your first investment in real estate. If you want to purchase a property, you can use debt by taking a mortgage out of that property, as though you already own it. This is often called "leverage," and it attracts many real estate investors because it allows them to acquire properties that they could not afford to buy otherwise. However, there are no guarantees in life, so using debt to purchase real estate can turn to disaster in a failing real estate market because the investor will still be required to make all mortgage payments, and that road can lead to bankruptcy.

As previously discussed, one of the main benefits of real estate investing vs. the stock market is the ability to acquire an investment property with relatively little money down and borrow the rest. But just like any other loan, this does require you to find somebody (usually a bank) who will lend you the money you need to start your investment career. That is why this chapter will focus on maximizing your borrowing potential.

First and foremost, take a realistic look at your finances. How much extra income do you actually have? Investing in any market is a gamble. If it was foolproof, the world would be made of millionaires. Make sure that you can afford to lose any money that you invest, and, especially when investing in real estate, make sure you will be able to afford to pay all of the monthly costs that come with owning that property until you find a tenant; this could take months in some cases.

Claim every penny of income that you can throughout the year, even cash payments. Of course, it is tempting not to report certain income, even if not legal, and nobody enjoys paying taxes if they can avoid it. But when it comes to trying to borrow money from a bank, that will seriously limit your borrowing potential. All the bank cares about is whether you can pay back their money. More income means you are a better credit risk. Plain and simple.

Banks don't just go back a couple of months when evaluating a loan request; they go back a couple of years. The more money you are reporting as income the more favorably they will view your request. Of course, you must pay taxes on any declared income, but you will seem stabler and like a better risk.

Reduce your available credit. As strange as it sounds, having a high credit limit with credit cards can hurt your borrowing potential.

Let's say that you have $40,000 in available credit spread out over several credit cards. You don't actually use the cards; you just have them in case of emergency. These high limits will actually lower your borrowing potential with banks. Why? Because even if you have not spent one dollar with these credit cards, the bank sees them as $40,000 in debt, because at any time after the loan is issued you *could* use them, and now you have an additional $40,000 in debt versus likely a similar amount of income.

Even making minimum payments on the credit cards at around 3% that is an additional $1,200 of expense for you each month So, banks err on the side of caution and treat that *potential* debt as a real debt; in other words, they take that $1,200 dollars away from your money available to repay their loan. This, of course, results in a smaller loan. So, if you have credit cards that you don't need, either pay them down or get rid of them altogether. This simple step will make you look much more attractive to lenders.

Make sure your tax returns are correct. As already discussed, banks look at the last two tax returns to determine your income. If your taxes are correct, up to date and include all income, this will show you as a stable person with a steady income—exactly the kind of folks banks want to lend to.

Split your expenses with your partner. If you have a partner whose name is not going to be on the mortgage, it can often be helpful to split expenses with them. Instead of paying for all of the monthly bills, allow your partner to pay for half of them. This will indicate to banks that your monthly expenses have room for a higher loan-repayment amount. There are some legalities when it comes to doing this, so make sure you speak with a tax accountant or a similar professional before getting started.

Find a lender who specializes in your kind of income. There are numerous ways to make a legitimate living. Not everyone has a nine-to-five job Monday through Friday. There are contractors, small business owners, Uber drivers, and the list goes on and on. Different lenders favor different types of income.

When choosing a lender, make sure you find one that specializes in your type of income. Otherwise, you are reducing the amount of money you will be able to borrow.

Find a lender who takes rental income into consideration. Unfortunately, not all banks or lenders will take rental income from an investment property into account. Some count none of the rent, others will take a very small percentage into consideration, but some will take 80% or more into account. Obviously, the more of the rent they will take into account as a means of repayment the higher the loan amount you will qualify for. So, we are beginning to see that the choice of lender can be a crucial one, in more ways than one.

Shop around for your loan. Finding the right lender is critical as well because you want to find the lowest interest rate you can. Every 1% of interest equals

$1,000 per year for every $100,000 of the loan. That is money you could be using to pay off the loan early or to invest in new properties. Therefore, it is well worth the investment of time to shop around until finding the best interest rate you can.

Find the right type of loan for you. As strange as it sounds, even within the same bank or lending institution the interest rates can vary based on the type of loan you take out. The best way to look into this is to speak to your banker or mortgage broker about what your borrowing potential will be with each type of loan.

Use other properties as collateral. If you own other properties, include them in the mortgage as collateral. This will give banks the peace of mind of knowing they can recoup their losses if everything goes belly up on the loan. Of course, this is also a risky strategy because, if the real estate market shifts against you, the bank could force you to sell the property to service the loan.

Another great strategy can be an interest-only loan. With interest loans, the borrower is allowed for a set period of time (5–10 years, usually, in the US) to pay only the interest on the mortgage. This means a lower monthly payment, so it will allow you to finance more debt under this strategy than if you had to repay the interest and principal in the beginning. This sort of loan is riskier for lenders, so they will usually charge a slightly higher interest rate.

This can also be accomplished by extending the length of the mortgage with a traditional principal and interest model. The monthly payment for a 30-year loan will be lower than a 20-year loan, which will again raise your borrowing potential.

Roll credit card debt into your mortgage. This is a risky strategy that can be more expensive in the long run, but another effective strategy can be to roll all of your credit card debt into a mortgage. If you are paying 20% on your credit card debt but only 5% on your mortgage, that extra 15% will show up to lenders as money that can be used to repay their loan, thus increasing your borrowing potential. This should not be done, however, if you are planning on keeping the property long term because over the life of the mortgage you will pay much more in interest than you would have had you simply paid off the credit card debt over 3–5 years. Additionally, if you default on credit card debt, the worst the lender can do is ding your credit report and pester you with phone calls; if you default on a mortgage, they can take your house away. However, if this is a short-term investment, such as a fix and flip, this can be a great strategy.

Save up your money for a larger down payment. While it may not be fast, this is a fantastic way to maximize your borrowing potential. If you can only put up less than 20% of the value of the property, you will be required to buy Private Mortgage Insurance (PMI). This is insurance to cover any losses to the lender if you are unable to service the debt and the lender cannot recoup all of their investment in a sale. The banks will take this cost into account when calculating how much debt you can afford to service, so if you can save up 21% of the cost as a deposit, that will do away with the need to pay for PMI every month and increase your borrowing power.

While you're saving up your money for the down payment on a property, how should you invest that money to earn a return on it? The answer is *don't*. Don't risk this money; this is your real estate future. Instead, put your money somewhere safe, like a federally insured bank. This is the time to practice something called capital preservation.

More people lose their money trying to squeeze a couple extra percentage points of profit out of it than by any other mistake. When it comes to money that you need for a specific purpose, such as your down payment, you must always keep your eye on the prize. Don't get distracted by shiny, new investments.

These savings need to be readily accessible to you within a few days at the most. This is money that is not supposed to be earning a return because it is designated for a specific purpose and you don't want to risk it. Your *extra* money is what is supposed to grow your wealth. This is called capital. It's the money you have set aside for investment purposes.

For example, the money you put into your 401(k) at work every month would be considered retirement capital as it is set aside to finance your retirement. The money you save at work through a 401(k) or 403(b) plan, for instance, would be considered retirement capital.

Most financial catastrophes have arisen from a well-meant decision to take on more financial risk than the investor could afford. It's easy to talk yourself into, and when you overextend yourself you are certain that it will all work out, but what if it doesn't? What if it goes wrong? The consequences will be financially devastating.

So, where should you keep your down payment? There are really only a few options to keep your money safe until the magical day when you have enough to begin your career as a real estate investor:

FDIC Insured Banks

You can put your money in a checking or savings account at any FDIC member bank. Your bank is almost certainly an FDIC member, and if you are not sure, look for the sticker on their window or just ask. The benefits of a bank are that you can access your money anytime during normal banking hours and there is no penalty for taking it out. Plus, if the bank fails, your money is completely insured by the government, up to $100,000.

FDIC Insured Certificates of Deposit (CDs)

CDs are offered by many FDIC members, such as local banks. A certificate of deposit is essentially a loan by you to the bank for a specific length of time in exchange for a guaranteed return on your investment. Normally, the rewards will be higher when the loan is for a longer period of time. If you are not going to be needing your money for a while, this can be a good option while offering higher returns than a simple bank account.

This is a poor choice if there is a possibility that you will need your money sooner than the duration of the loan to the bank. If you do withdraw your money early, there can be significant financial penalties, so make sure you will not need that money until the CD expires.

U.S. Treasury Bills (T-Bills)

T-Bills are debts from the US government that mature after one year or less. T-Bills are considered absolutely safe because they are fully backed by the United States government so a default is unthinkable. Treasury bills are sold at a lower rate than face value, but once they mature you receive the full face value. This only really makes sense for larger amounts of money over $10,000.

Money Market Accounts

A Money Market Account (MMA) is nothing more than a savings account at your local bank. (MMAs are *not* the same as a Money Market Fund, which is a sort of mutual fund investment.) MMAs typically earn a much higher interest rate than a traditional savings account because you are authorizing the bank to use that money for its own investments. The ability to transfer that money is a little more limited, but since you are not going to be using that money it should not matter. There is a minimum deposit required from $500 all the way up to $5,000. These accounts are usually FDIC insured, just like any other savings account, which protects you if your bank fails. Before investing in an MMA, **always** double check with your bank that it is FDIC insured; if not, keep looking.

U.S. Savings Bonds

There are two main types of United States savings bonds: Series I and Series EE. Each has its own benefits, but if you don't need your money for at least a year, they may be ideal for you because you are guaranteed never to lose money on your investment. This is the peace of mind you need when you are storing money that you need, like that down payment for your real estate dreams.

Chapter 3

Protecting Your Assets

Real estate is a risky business and, above all, your personal assets must be protected. If somebody gets personally injured due to a defect in one of your buildings, you don't want them to be able to sue you personally. This first part is very important, and it will be repeated. You do not invest in real estate in your own name when purchasing properties. Not ever, if you can avoid it. Instead, to protect your personal wealth, look into forming a legal structure known as an LLC, or Limited Liability Company, or another form of limited partnership. Usually, when something goes wrong, only the assets of the LLC or of the partnership can be forfeited, not those of the members. So, if, for example, one of your investments goes belly up or someone slips and falls in your business, the worst case scenario is that you lose your investment, not everything you own. This is why I will stress *do not buy real estate investments in your own name!*

Recently, such Limited Liability Companies have become popular methods for small investors to own parts of family businesses or new companies. The protections and benefits they provide to the members of the LLC leave no doubt as to why they have exploded in popularity among investors. As a new investor, it is crucial for you to understand LLCs and how they will impact your taxes.

So, what exactly is an LLC? In a nutshell, a Limited Liability Company is a sort of cross between a partnership and a corporation. You get the simplicity and tax breaks of a partnership with all the personal asset protection of a corporation.

The owners of a Limited Liability Company are referred to officially as the "members". A Limited Liability Company can have one member or many, as many as you want. Under an LLC structure, the members' personal assets are protected from being seized by the company's debt holders.

LLCs are relatively new entities, only appearing for the first time around four decades ago. Today, they are the fastest growing type of new business entity. We will discuss the pros and cons of forming an LLC to help you decide whether it is right for you.

Limited Liability Company pros:

There are a number of advantages to structuring your company as an LLC. These include:

Limited Liability

Members cannot be held personally liable for any actions that the company takes. As previously discussed, this means that, as a member of an LLC, your personal assets (cars, bank accounts, 401(k), your home) are safe if the company owes money to a creditor. If you decide that a Limited Liability Company is the right option for you, make sure you keep your personal and business finances totally separate and run your company legitimately because you could lose this protection otherwise.

Pass-Through Federal Taxation

By default, a Limited Liability Company is considered by the IRS to be a pass-through entity. This means that any profits will go straight to the members without being taxed at the corporate level by the government. Instead, members declare these profits on their personal income tax returns. This makes filing taxes much simpler, and if there are no profits, members can list those losses to offset their tax burdens.

Simple to Get Started

Compared to forming a new corporation, forming a Limited Liability Company is quite easy and the fees are much lower, though this does vary state by state. You should absolutely consult with an attorney or an accountant to make sure that a Limited Liability Company is a good option for your individual circumstances, but once you decide to form one, you should be able to manage the paperwork without an outside specialist. This will save you more money to invest in a down payment.

You Can Manage It Yourself

One of the problems with a corporation is that it must be managed by an elected board of directors. This problem is completely solved by a Limited Liability Company. This is because a Limited Liability Company offers much greater flexibility when deciding what sort of management you would like to have running your company. You can decide that the LLC will be managed by its members (you, in other words) or you can choose to bring in professional managers from outside if you prefer to be more hands-off. Some states even consider a Limited Liability Company member-managed by default, unless the LLC's filings with the state request otherwise. Remember, a Limited Liability Company can even consist of only one member, so if you prefer to give no other member control over how your money is invested, you can be the only member of the Limited Liability Company. This is not recommended, however, because it will limit the pool of money that is available to be invested in your extra income.

Limited Liability Company cons:

We can see that a Limited Liability Company has some significant advantages, but it may not be right for every investor. There are some drawbacks, so before you decide how you're going to organize your company, let's discuss some of them.

Membership Turnover Has Consequences

This is one of the more problematic drawbacks of a Limited Liability Company. There are many states in the US where if a member dies, goes bankrupt or otherwise leaves the company, the Limited Liability Company itself must be completely broken up, and the remaining members must fulfill any remaining financial or legal obligations necessary to dissolve the business. The remaining members can still do business, naturally, but they will have to form an entirely new Limited Liability Company to do so as before.

A Limited Liability Company Does Have Limits

Even if your company has been set up as a Limited Liability Company, the courts can still decide that your Limited Liability Company cannot protect your personal assets. If you are not careful to keep your business finances separate from your personal finances, or if the judge decides that you have run your company fraudulently and harmed others by doing so, the courts can "pierce the corporate veil," meaning your personal assets can be seized. So, if you do decide to organize your company under a Limited Liability Company, make sure you keep your financial transactions separate and always act in good faith with those you are doing business with. (Good advice in daily life too.)

Taxes

Unless the Limited Liability Company requests otherwise, the IRS will consider the company as a partnership for tax purposes unless the company chooses to be taxed as a corporation. What this means is that the members working for the Limited Liability Company are considered to be self-employed. Those self-employed members are fully responsible for paying Medicare and Social Security taxes personally. This is known as self-employment tax, and members are taxed based upon the Limited Liability Company's net profits if any. However, if your Limited Liability Company chooses to be taxed as an S Corporation, members who work for the company are only taxed based upon your actual compensation from the company, not the company's net earnings. Which of these options will work best for your particular circumstances must be discussed by you and a qualified accountant.

Getting Started

Once you have decided whether a Limited Liability Company is the right choice for you, it is quite easy to get started.

First, simply choose a name for your company. Register a name that has not already been used in the state where you plan to do business. You can use online searches, the county clerk and your state's secretary of state to make sure that your name has not already been taken. Make sure you do this in all states where you plan to do business.

Next, select a registered agent for your Limited Liability Company. This is the person the members select to represent the Limited Liability Company in all official correspondence. Most states require the name and address of the registered agent be listed on the filing application as all official correspondence will be addressed to that person. Your Limited Liability Company may choose to have a member serve in this capacity in most states or you may choose to hire a third-party company that specializes in registered-agent services.

Third, draw up your partnership agreement. If you are the only member of the Limited Liability Company, you may skip this step, but most readers will be interested in pooling their resources with other like-minded investors, and this step is crucial. It is not required by law, but you and the other members should certainly develop a written agreement that outlines exactly how the company will be managed, who owns what percentage of the company, voting structures, who will be responsible for what duties within the company, profit and loss distribution, etc. In other words, try to solve any potential problems in advance in writing with the other members so that everyone is on the same page from day one. This will help to avoid difficult conversations between the members down the road.

After that, file your articles of organization. This is what will make your Limited Liability Company official in the state's eyes. Most states require basic information such as the name, management type, principal place of business, etc. If you have planned your business thoroughly, these questions will present no problem.

Obtain your employer ID number. Since you will be operating as a partnership if you elect to set up a Limited Liability Company, the IRS will require you to have an EIN. This number will be required by the IRS for tax purposes, so don't forget this step!

Finally, we have already discussed the potential risks involved if you mix up your business and personal financial transactions as a member of a Limited Liability Company. To help avoid this, set up a business checking account with your bank. As long as this account is only used for business transactions, it should be much easier to make sure your finances are kept separate.

It can certainly be scary to do business in our litigious society today, but as we can see, if you take a few simple steps and manage your business in good faith, a small business setback does not have to automatically mean personal financial ruin as well.

Chapter 4

Direct Ownership Real Estate Investment

We have briefly touched on the various ways to invest in real estate, and in the next chapters, we will discuss several of these options in depth. Real estate is one of the oldest forms of investment and is still as popular as ever. But most new real estate investors have no idea how many different ways there are to invest in real estate. Each investment type has its pros and cons, of course, and this book will give you a leg up on the competition since you will learn about many of them that your competition simply has not.

One of the best ways to build fortune is to find a niche and stick to it. Among the first lessons of business is not to try to be all things to all people; find what you excel at in business and stick to that.

But, before we dive in, another word of caution about protecting your money. *All* investment comes with risk; that's why it's not just called "free money." To state it one more time, you should almost never buy investment real estate properties in your own name; use a Limited Liability Company or any other structure that will protect your personal assets if the worst should happen!

With that out of the way again, let's dive right into this fascinating world.

Perhaps the most common type of real estate investment and the one most familiar to the new investor is called direct ownership real estate investment. This type of investment involves the highest potential reward but also the highest risk. It is also the most hands-on of the investment types, so if you are looking for a completely passive income, this may not be the strategy for you.

From apartment buildings to business complexes, you can find the kind of direct ownership investment property that fits you and your budget. The basic premise of direct ownership investment is that you purchase or build some piece of real estate and the difference between the cost of ownership of that property and the income from those occupying and using the property represents your profit or loss. That is the simplest description of this type of investment, but there may be more opportunities for direct ownership than you imagined.

Residential investments can include a house, an apartment building, a condo, a vacation home or any other property where someone will pay you to let them live on the property. Most of these are governed by an agreement between the tenant and the owner (or manager) called a "lease." A lease defines how long the tenant may occupy the property and how much they will pay for that, as well as any other responsibilities or rights that the tenant may have. Most leases in the US are for 12 months, which gives you the benefit of knowing how much you will receive from that property for 12 months, but if the market explodes in that area, you may not be able to take advantage of the increased earning potential during the lifetime of the lease.

Business real estate investments can include properties like strip malls, shopping malls or any other retail storefront. Not only can the owner of these types of property receive a monthly payment from the tenant in exchange for occupying the property, but many owners also receive a percentage of any sales generated by the tenant's business. This offsets the cost to the owner of keeping up the property and keeping it looking great.

Commercial real estate includes things like skyscrapers, office buildings, converted office spaces, etc. For an investor, these investments can be very appealing because often numerous companies will set up their offices within a single building, thus doing away with the risk to the owner of the building that he or she will receive no rent if one company goes belly up. In addition, commercial real estate usually involves multi-year leases, as opposed to only 12 months, which is customary in residential real estate. This comes with the same caveat as residential real estate in the case of the market heating up in that area, but the stable cash flow generated by multi-year leases makes up for that with many investors. In addition, in both commercial and residential real estate, a lease will also protect the investor against potential *declining* rental rates in the area.

Mixed-use real estate investments are gaining favor in many larger cities. These include any combination of the above-listed real estate investment types. In many cities, it is not uncommon to see a storefront on the ground floor of a building, offices on the middle floors, and private residences on the upper floors. As an investor, you will have an income stream from all of these sources. For larger investors, this can include setting up a large office complex with several commercial buildings surrounding it, such as restaurants, to serve the employees who work in the office complex. The appeal of mixed-use real estate investment is obvious due to the diversity of the income streams, but this type of investment usually requires significant resources, more than the typical investor will initially have.

Industrial real estate investments can include everything from a car lot or a car wash to a large warehouse leased by a company to distribute its product or any other special purpose property generating income from customers using that property. These types of investments often come with additional revenue streams, such as coin-operated vending machines, vacuum cleaners at a car wash, arcade video games—all of which maximize the investors' return.

These are the most obvious forms of direct ownership real estate investment, but there are several other ways to profit from investing in direct ownership of a real estate property. Many small investors, for example, will purchase a small apartment complex, such as a duplex or fourplex, and live in one unit while renting the other(s) out. This usually does not result in much, if any, direct profit, but the rental income will help build equity while you are living there for free. In the future, once the mortgage has been fully paid, most of the rental income will become a direct profit for you. Buying a piece of real estate or a building and then leasing it back to a tenant, such as a business, is more like a fixed income investment than an actual real estate investment. Basically, you are financing a building and allowing the income from the tenants to build equity for you.

Building equity in real estate is great, but it is not the only important thing to consider. You should never sacrifice liquidity in an attempt to build equity. This is a very easy way to end up in bankruptcy court. This can best be illustrated with two examples.

Let's imagine two homeowners—Holly and Mike. Now, Mike and Holly are like most Americans; they both want to own a home outright. This is the American dream, after all. But we will show you how it can be *disadvantageous* to make overpayments on your mortgage unless you are in a position to pay it off completely.

One of the most important lessons in business, or in life in general, is to keep enough cash on hand to withstand any setback, whether it be an illness or an economic downturn. Having this cash on hand is called being "liquid." As an investor, remaining liquid is vital.

Now, let's say you own the bank that holds the mortgages for Holly and Mike. Both own houses valued at $250,000. Well, Mike has never been a very good customer of your bank. He is up to his neck in credit card debt, has high car payments, is not always employed and is generally not liquid.

Holly, however, has been a dream customer. She has an outstanding credit score and often makes double payments or even triple payments on her mortgage. But Holly is not very liquid either.

Due to their differing payment habits, Mike still owes $200,000 on his house, and Holly only owes about $20,000 more. Both are eagerly awaiting the day when they will own their homes free and clear, but Holly is much closer to the goal.

But, catastrophe strikes both. For whatever reason, both are now out of work and are struggling to make ends meet each month. As the holder of their mortgages, your bank does not know that any of this has happened. All the bank knows is that it should receive a payment from Mike and Holly by their respective due dates and for the correct amounts.

As the mortgage holder, your alarms should start to go off after about 2 missed payments. Of course, as a human being, you feel for their hardship, and you want to help, but at the end of the day, you are investing other people's hard-earned money, and you have an obligation to the investors to manage their money responsibly.

Eventually, the time comes when banking regulations require you to acknowledge that you are unlikely to be paid any further by either Mike or Holly. This is not good for the bank. The bank's profitability is damaged, the balance sheet has two large outstanding debts, and the investors are expecting you to act to protect their money. So, what do you do?

Your job, as the owner of the bank, is to get these loans back into the black as soon as possible. This is mostly accomplished by foreclosing on the property and auctioning it in an attempt to recoup your losses.

However, here is where things become counter-intuitive. For who is more likely to be foreclosed upon—Mike, who is a financial shambles and has very little equity in his home, or Holly, who made so many overpayments? Unfortunately, from a math perspective, this is an easy decision.

To recoup your losses on Mike's house, you would have to sell it for almost the full original loan amount of $250,000 to break even after the costs of the foreclosure, listing the house, auction fees, etc. At best, it will be a lengthy process to break even, and when it comes to your balance sheet, time is of the essence. Since Holly has made so many overpayments, she now only owes $20,000 on a house that was originally purchased for $250,000. If you foreclose on her, you can sell that property quickly at a very steep discount and recoup your $20,000 in bad debt.

Naturally, you feel for Holly and acknowledge that she did everything right, and perhaps it is not fair that she is the one to lose her house, and Mike is more likely to have his loan restructured on easier terms for him, but from an investment perspective it makes perfect sense. Investors are not only millionaires looking to increase their wealth, but they also consist of 401(k) and IRA retirement funds. Your duty to these investors is to guarantee them a stable return on their investments.

Letting Mike's house sit around on the market for months so that you can make little to no profit, and potentially lose money on the deal, is not good for your investors. Selling Holly's house on the market for 50% of its original selling price, on the other hand, should take only several weeks and ensures that your investors have recouped their money. Holly will lose a great deal more of her equity than if she had had time to list it herself on the market for a fair price, but the bank's balance sheet will remain clean.

The sad fact is the bank is going after Holly's house first. As Mike's lender, you know you are unlikely to achieve anything positive by going after his house, so you are more likely to work with him and restructure his payments somehow to keep his loan in good standing on the books. There are regulations specifying how far the bank can go to legitimately keep Mike's loan on the books as a "good" loan, but within this framework, it is up to the bank how far it is willing to go to avoid having to write off this bad debt.

For both Mike and Holly, this could have been avoided by staying liquid. Never forget, the bank is not concerned with how much money you still owe them; it just wants its monthly payments, on time and in full, so that the loan remains healthy on the books.

Rather than making so many double and triple payments, Holly would have done better to put that money into a safe low-yield investment. This way, when disaster struck, she would have been able to withdraw those funds and continue to make her monthly payments with that money until she was back on her feet. And if it turned out that she would not be able to get back on her feet, she would have been able to sell the house at a fair market price, repay the bank the remainder of the loan, and pocket any remaining equity before the worst happened.

The danger of being liquid, however, is the temptation to spend that money. It is hard to avoid being tempted by an account with a large amount of money in it that is not designated for any other purpose. The desire will always be there to just dip a little into that account for other purposes and replace it later. The problem with this is that for most folks the replacement will never happen but the debt remains.

Liquidity is a vital strategy, but, as we can see, it requires a great deal of discipline. If you decide to take my advice and set aside money for a rainy day each month, which I hope you do, consider that money gone once it has been placed into your reserve fund, wherever you choose to store that money. Don't be tempted to take out "just a little" to spend on anything other than a house payment in an emergency situation. This is all that money should be used for.

Another danger of that rainy day fund is the temptation to make riskier investments to maximize your returns. But remember, this is not your investment capital; this is your emergency reserve. It is not meant to generate a large return, it is meant to be *there and safe* in the event you need it.

As an investor, one of the worst things that could happen is that you lose your investment because, due to a temporary hardship, you were unable to make the monthly payments on the property that was supposed to build the foundation of your financial future. Please don't be that investor; remain liquid above nearly all else and don't touch your rainy day fund, unless it is raining *hard*.

Fix and Flip

With the explosion in popularity of reality TV personalities purchasing rundown houses, fixing them up, and then quickly flipping them for a tidy profit, "house flipping" has become one of the most common forms of direct ownership real estate investment, so much so that we will devote a much longer section to this topic.

First lesson, don't believe the hype. No matter what you see on TV, learning to fix and flip houses is neither easy nor quick, although it can be quite profitable. House flipping actually requires a fair amount of knowledge—much more than can be gained from taking a two-day course and watching reality TV—and a lot of work.

However, it can be done successfully, and, as with anything, the best way to learn is to do it. You will make mistakes, and you will learn from those and get better next time. It's how we learn. As long as you have followed my recommendation to protect yourself, your downside risk should be minimized. Is it easy to flip houses? Nope. But there are certain common mistakes that I will share here to help you avoid the major pitfalls and still walk away with a nice return. And, of course, the more you do it the better you will be at it.

What Exactly Is House Flipping?

Before we get into the actual process of house flipping, let's just take a closer look at what it actually is. The term "flipping houses" is used by most people to refer to the process of buying distressed properties at foreclosure auctions or short sales at a steep discount. As mentioned above, the bank is just trying to recoup its investment as fast as possible, so sale prices are usually well below market value. The investor will then quickly resell ("flip") the property to a homeowner closer to market value without doing many, if any, renovations. This is what house flipping actually is, and it can be profitable, but that's not the kind of house flipping we will discuss. That kind of house flipping relies on quick turnover and quick profits to be effective.

Wholesaling of real estate is often, wrongly, also referred to as flipping houses. The wholesaling of real estate is a process whereby the wholesaler makes a contract with a home seller to purchase the home and then "flips" that contract to a real estate investor for a profit. In other words, the wholesaler simply inserts himself as a middleman between buyer and seller. As a real estate investor, you may find real estate wholesalers to be a valuable asset, but this is also not the sort of flipping we will discuss.

Learning real estate investment, including house flipping, is not easy. It takes a lot of capital and a lot of hard work. In the sort of house flipping we will discuss here, you will need capital for the initial purchase of the property and capital to renovate the property to add value and maximize your return. Done correctly, this can be quite a great investment, but in the wrong market or with bad luck, it can also be risky.

One final word of caution before we dive in here: many contractors think that they can make their fortunes with house flipping, but this may be because their math is flawed. Contractors often make the mistake of investing their capital in a house, doing the remodel themselves, selling the property, and then counting the difference between what they invested and what they sold the property for as their profit.

The problem with this is that the contractor is not taking his *risk* into consideration. Let's say a contractor takes on a job for a real estate investor, for example, that would take 8 weeks and net him $30,000 in profit. This contractor has kept his employees busy for 8 weeks and had made $30,000 for his investment of time and resources. Now, let's say that the same contractor bought a distressed property, had his crew work on it for 8 weeks, and then resold the property for a $30,000 profit. The contractor has actually achieved nothing, except to put his money at risk. See, the contractor put his own capital at risk to invest in the project and made only the same amount of money he would have made by working for the real estate investor, whose job it is to put capital at risk.

So, if you are a contractor reading this because you want to move into real estate investing, make sure you will make more money flipping the house than you would have by simply being hired to do the remodel.

Now, the first step to successfully flipping houses profitably is to know where you stand financially. It is crucial to know exactly how much money you will have available to invest in your property and to renovate it and whether you will need to borrow money or take on investment partners to raise enough capital.

Finding investors is, of course, not always easy, but knowing what your financial situation is in advance is the most logical place to get started. Initially, to minimize your personal risk, you will want to invest as little of your own money as possible. Of course, this will dilute the profits that you will get personally, but it is far better to get only a share of the profits than nothing at all. Additionally, taking on a partner or investor who has experience with flipping houses will provide you with another resource to avoid the most devastating pitfalls.

The next step is to build a team you trust. This is the team that will help you find the properties, fix them up, and then sell them for a (hopefully) nice profit.

It is simply impossible to complete a house flip all by yourself and still remain profitable. So, build a dream team to help you wade through it faster than you could by yourself; you will then also have a team to put your head together with when things go wrong.

At first, your team (at a minimum) should consist of a real estate broker, a contractor, architect, accountant, money lender and your insurance expert. The collective wisdom of this team should make you profitable much faster than you could hope to achieve on your own. This is not the time to be stubborn or greedy. Bringing in help will make your life easier, no matter what level of experience you possess, and will make the ultimate profits much greater.

The next step is an obvious one but is easier said than done. You must find a suitable property to flip. If you have taken the valuable step of doing your homework and finding the most promising neighborhood to invest in, this will make your task even more challenging as your choice will be limited to that geographic area, but the right neighborhood can make or break an investment, so don't skimp on the homework.

The goal is to buy a property for a low price, accurately assess the remodel costs, and then sell it for a worthwhile profit. This is why you will need your team. The faster you can work your way through all these steps the more properties you will flip and the more money you will ultimately make.

A real estate broker or a real estate wholesaler will be critical resources in helping you find properties that will sell cheaply enough for you to make a profit.

I cannot stress this part enough: do the math. Like contractors forgetting to take their risk factor into account, more house flippers have been undone by flawed math than nearly any other factor.

When choosing whether to invest your money into a property, you will want to take a hardheaded look at the numbers. Make a realistic assessment of what the house will cost to obtain initially, how much it will cost to repair the home (here I always recommend budgeting for the worst-case scenario; this is not the time for wishful thinking), and what the house is likely to sell for once it has been renovated. As you are doing your math, don't forget to take into account the monthly costs of owning the house, such as taxes, maintenance fees, etc., until you can sell it.

If you have crunched all of these numbers together with your team and everybody agrees that you will make enough money off your collective investment to make it worthwhile, you have likely found your winner, and you should consider making an offer on it.

Another common mistake that flippers make is not managing the renovation with a tight leash. You should not micromanage your contractor, you chose that person for a reason, and you should trust them to handle and supervise the repairs; but it is your job to keep an eye on the repairs to ensure they are being done efficiently and on-budget.

The initial purchase price of the house will play a large role in your ultimate profits, but if you keep an eye on the renovations and your budget, this will make sure you get the full potential out of the house when you finally sell it.

In addition to letting your contractor work unsupervised, the second major mistake investors make when renovating their properties is over-renovating. At the end of the day, you are not going to be living in this home; you should not decorate it to suit your tastes. Your goal is to make the house desirable and profitable, so unless doing something to the house will make it significantly more valuable on the market, don't bother.

You must also know your market when it comes to managing the renovation. Even if a particular improvement would increase the value of the house by thousands of dollars, it may not be worth doing if the other houses in the neighborhood are not selling for as much money as you would hope to receive if you undertook that improvement.

Finally, the last tip when it comes to flipping houses is to work fast. Your profit depends on how fast you work. The longer your renovation takes and the longer your house sits on the market waiting for a buyer the smaller your profits. Every month that goes by sees more and more money out of your pocket for taxes, insurance costs, mortgage payments, utilities, and on and on. It all adds up, so the faster you can turn that house over the more profit you will ultimately make.

This does not mean you should do shoddy work or cut corners. Your workmanship should reflect your personal values and should add value to the property; the work should just be done as fast as possible.

Every property is different, of course, but you should budget for about 6 months from purchase to sale, with a few extra months of expenses added on to be on the safe side. So, make sure you can afford to wait that long for a return on your investment.

Many investors make the mistake of believing that house flipping can only be profitable in times of rapid real estate appreciation, but this is simply not so. If you choose your properties wisely, work quickly and efficiently while still putting out a product you can be proud of, fixing and flipping will always be a profitable endeavor for you.

Chapter 5

Real Estate Investment Groups and Limited Partnerships

A real estate investment group is simply that—a group of partners who invest in real estate. This is similar to direct ownership real estate investment but is structured in a way that is less hands-on for the investor.

The different types of investments that are available to a real estate investment group are much the same as those available to a single investor. The difference lies in the fact that a real estate investment group provides only the capital investment.

They will usually hire a property management company to manage the properties for the investors in exchange for a percentage of the monthly income from the properties. When choosing your property management, choose wisely because your investment is only going to be as good as the people managing it.

These groups will also often serve as money lenders to established flippers who wish to take on a larger project. Here, too, the group will leave the day-to-day operations to the experts in exchange for a share of the profits.

For many investors who desire a less hands-on approach to investing but don't want to simply hand their money over to a mutual fund or some other sort of investment firm and passively observe the results, this can be an ideal option.

The profit margin will be smaller, of course, since investors must pay the experts to carry out day-to-day operations for them, but the risk is also significantly less than being a sole investor because it is spread out among a group of investors who allow real estate professionals to manage their investments for them.

There are many real estate investment groups out there to choose from. As always, it is your hard-earned money that you are investing, so it is your responsibility to do your homework and make sure you are choosing a real estate investment group that fits your needs and whose investments match the level of risk that you are looking for.

Many investors choose to form their own Real estate investment group by finding a group of like-minded friends to pool their resources with. When forming your group, it will be important for you to make sure that everybody is on the same page.

Another key point to remember is to make sure to keep a reserve of funds to cover the costs associated with any long-term vacant units. You don't want to lose your investment for lack of a couple hundred dollars a month.

Real estate limited partnerships can be another great investment opportunity if you are not looking to be a landlord. Real estate limited partnerships essentially invest money in developing new real estate properties, and the profit represents the difference between the cost of building the property and the price it eventually sells for.

These partnerships require little to no hands-on involvement, other than perhaps occasional meetings, and do not require you to be a landlord and deal with everything that comes along with that, although the profit will, again, be smaller.

Chapter 6

Real Estate Investment Trusts

Not every investor wants to be even that hands-on with their real estate investments; many are looking for more of a passive investment. One of the more popular investments in the real estate investing community is called a Real Estate Investment Trust or REIT.

Real Estate Investment Trusts can be a convenient option for the average investor to profit from the real estate market without having to deal with the headache of direct property acquisition.

Prior to the 1960s, only the wealthiest individuals and corporations were in a financial position to invest in larger real estate projects, such as shopping malls, business complexes, hotels, skyscrapers, etc. Finally, with the Real Estate Investment Trust Act of 1960, Congress made these special companies exempt from corporate income taxes if they met certain conditions.

The reason Congress passed this was in an attempt to create an incentive for investors to pool their resources in the form of companies investing in large real estate projects. It was successful as the first Real Estate Investment Trust was created only three years later.

In exchange for these generous tax breaks, Real Estate Investment Trusts must pass a fourfold test each year to maintain their status.

First, the trust must distribute at least 90% of its annual taxable income, except for capital gains, each year to its shareholders as dividends.

Second, the trust must have at least 75% of its assets invested in real estate, though this can also include investing in other Real Estate Investment Trusts, mortgage loans, and government securities.

Third, the trust must obtain 75% of its income from real estate, including rents, interest from mortgage loans or profits from selling real estate.

Finally, the Real Estate Investment Trust must have at least 100 shareholders, and no small group of shareholders can own more than half of the shares. The regulations forbid a group of five shareholders or less from owning more than 50% of all shares. This prevents too much influence from collecting in the hands of a powerful few.

One of the benefits of investing in a Real Estate Investment Trust is that REITs are required by regulations to distribute almost all of their income (at least 90%) as dividends. This does come with some tax implications for you as an investor, however; for example, your dividends will be taxed at a higher rate than common stocks, but this can be a great addition to your investment portfolio if you can buy in at the right price and have enough margin of safety.

Another advantage is that you can avoid double-taxation, allowing more investor capital to compound.

You will have a professional, dedicated management team running the day-to-day operations of the business in a way that would perhaps exceed your personal level of expertise.

Unlike directly-owned real estate, Real Estate Investment Trusts are fairly liquid, meaning you can cash out quickly if necessary, while a house or condo may sit on the market for months before selling.

Due to their relatively high level of cash dividends compared to the market, Real Estate Investment Trusts provide more portfolio stability than many other investments because they are less likely to sink as low as common stock in the case of a market downturn.

Investing in Real Estate Investment Trusts, investors with only a few thousand dollars to invest can diversify their investment across different geographic areas or across different areas of specialization. Investing only in direct ownership, you would need a much larger pool of capital to accomplish this.

To get started investing in a Real Estate Investment Trust, simply decide what sort of real estate you would like to invest your money in, do your homework to find a REIT that matches your interests and will protect your money, and contact your broker about making the investment. If you do decide that investing in Real Estate Investment Trusts is right for you, just remember that REITs are not just a collection of real estate properties; they are actually businesses that you are investing in, so make sure you analyze them as such when doing your research.

Conclusion

Thank you for making it through to the end of this book, let's hope it was informative and able to provide you with all of the tools you need to achieve your goals whatever they may be.

The world of real estate investing is a fascinating one. Many fortunes have been made with a relatively small initial investment.

Real estate investment is perfect for those who are not looking to simply throw money at a professional broker to invest and hope for the best. It offers a great opportunity to invest your money with a good chance of making a decent return with you in charge of how your money is invested. Unless you choose to make your investment in a Real Estate Investment Trust or something similar, you will at least have some control over how your money is invested, and if you choose direct ownership, you will have complete control. The best part is there are investments for any level of involvement you're looking for, so if it's a totally passive income that you want, then a REIT may be perfect for you. After all, it's your money, and you should invest it in the way that makes you most comfortable.

With thousands of years of tradition backing it, property ownership can give you security, social standing, and, not least of all, a roof over your head.

And who doesn't want that? As an investor in real estate, not only can you hope to make a worthwhile profit from your investment, you can also help your buyers achieve *their* goal of property ownership.

There are few other investments that are quite so tangible or immediate as real estate. When you own a piece of property, you can visit it, touch it, show it to your friends; it is *there*. Many investors love this about real estate. The property is there as proof of your investment, and you get all the pride of ownership, even if you are not going to live in the property.

The next step is to get started! As with any game, you can only win if you are on the field, playing. And the more you play the better you will become.

Finally, if you found this book useful in any way, a review on Amazon is always appreciated!

www.ingramcontent.com/pod-product-compliance
Lightning Source LLC
Chambersburg PA
CBHW031428210526
45464CB00005B/2109